Conspiracies, Lies, & Hidden Agendas

Conspiracies, Lies, & Hidden Agendas

Mick Farren

RENAISSANCE BOOKS
Los Angeles

Library of Congress Catalog Card Number: 99-63045
ISBN: 1-58063-077-4

10 9 8 7 6 5 4 3 2 1
Design by Tanya Maiboroda
Icons created by James Tran and Lisa-Theresa Lenthall

Published by Renaissance Books
Distributed by St. Martin's Press
Manufactured in the United States of America
First Edition

To the memory of William S. Burroughs,
who taught me to be suspicious of everything.

HARPER : . . . maybe the doors will hold, or maybe the troubles will come and the sky will collapse and there will be terrible rains and showers of poisoned light, or maybe life is really fine . . . maybe it's even worse that I know, maybe . . . I want to know, maybe I don't. The suspense, Mr. Lies, is killing me.

MR. LIES : I suggest a vacation.

—Tony Kushner, *Angels in America—Part One: Millenium Approaches*

There's something addicting about a secret.

—J. Edgar Hoover

The obscure we see eventually. The completely apparent takes a little longer.

—Edward R. Murrow

Those who dream by night . . . wake to find that all was vanity, but the dreamers of the day are dangerous men, for they may act on their dreams with open eyes and make it all possible.

—T. E. Lawrence (Lawrence of Arabia)

When you have eliminated the impossible, whatever remains, however implausible, must be the truth.

—Sherlock Holmes in Sir Arthur Conan Doyle's *The Sign of Four*

If a nation expects to be ignorant and free in a state of civilization, it expects what never was and never will be.

—Thomas Jefferson

The great masses of the people will more easily fall victim to a great lie than to a small one.

—Adolf Hitler

If both the past and the external world exist only in the mind, and if the mind itself is controllable—what then?

—George Orwell

Recent history of mankind is the record of a vast conspiracy to impose one level of mechanical consciousness on mankind.

—**Allen Ginsberg**

It is possible that a certain amount of brain damage is of therapeutic value.

—**Dr. Paul Hoch**

Sacred cows make the tastiest hamburger.

—**Abbie Hoffman**

I'm just a patsy.

—**Lee Harvey Oswald**

This is the End, beautiful friend.

—**Jim Morrison**

What, me worry?

—**Alfred E. Neuman**

Contents

Introduction

The Need to Know

At one time or another, most of us have experienced the feeling that things were going on that we were not being told about, that things were happening in the world, in the government, in our own town and street, or out in the depths of the cosmos that might, sooner or later, directly affect or influence our lives. We could do nothing about this and were also kept totally in the dark. The feeling of being at the mercy of unknown forces has to be as old as humanity itself, and we have never liked it. We humans are a curious, inquisitive bunch. By our very nature, we are the monkeys who can't stand not to know. We have climbed mountains, crossed deserts, and sailed across oceans for scarcely more reason than to see what was on the other side. We have gazed at the motion of the stars and planets and watched the tides roll in and out. We have recorded, as best we could, the times at which the sun and moon rose and set. We have mapped and measured and undertaken seemingly impossible journeys. Much of human history is the story of people constantly on the move and constantly looking for answers, and when those answers are not forthcoming, theories and scenarios are made up to fill that unbearable void of ignorance.

Our ancient ancestors wondered what caused the thunder, why the rains came when they did, why sometimes the crops flourished and at other times failed; they puzzled over the true nature of sickness and death. They wove fantastic stories of what lay beyond the limits of their consciousness and perception. When no ready explanations presented themselves for random occurrences and accidents of fate, our forebears turned to the supernatural for the comfort of reasons why. They attempted to give credit or attach blame to all manner of unseen gods, spirits, and demons who either operated a system of mysterious rewards and punishments, or who simply amused themselves—much in the manner of the gods of ancient Greece—by capriciously interfering in human affairs for their own amusement.

In a lot of respects, we are not all that unlike our ancestors. Most of the time we live in the world of normality—of the routine and the daily grind—where we profoundly hope that nothing weird or untoward is going to occur. Every so often, however, we find ourselves glancing over our shoulders into that other place, the larger, wider, and less manageable world where all manner of strangeness is possible, where much is not what it appears, and we believe something's happening, but we don't know what it is. With each new backward glance, that macro-world grows more complex and more threatening. We discover that systems that we barely understand are increasingly ruling the essential details of our lives, that previously unknown diseases threaten our future, that new technologies are thrust on us unrequested and often unwanted. Change occurs constantly and at a frightening rate, and although—here in the U.S.A.—we supposedly live in a democracy, we rarely seem to be consulted about the great majority of these changes. As Marshall McLuhan predicted some thirty years ago, "we are in the speed-up."

Like the cop who tells the gawkers at a crime scene or traffic accident, "Move along now, there's nothing to see" when it's patently obvious that there's really plenty to see, those in authority tend to treat the public's access to information on a very limited "need to know" basis. Although it may not be right, part of this may be understandable. Since the end of World War II, and all through the nuclear tension of the Cold War, the world has spent a great deal of its time in a state of military preparedness and propagandist paranoia. The constant—if maybe less than rational—fear that Communist agents were everywhere gave rise to a cult of secrecy in which a whole spectrum of information was kept from the general public in what became known as "the interests of national security."

Unfortunately, the interests of national security were also used to cover a multitude of sins, and a good many of these sins were committed in those dark places where the machinations of politicians and generals interface with a vast and hugely profitable defense industry. This created serious doubts in the minds of many ordinary citizens and even in those of the more honorable in power. In his last act as president, Dwight Eisenhower warned the nation to beware of the military industrial complex and its war machine's potential for taking over the entire functioning of the country.

This cult of secrecy also didn't restrict itself to just the workings of the military industrial complex. In the private sector, in a mirror image of the defense contractors, many large corporations grew increasingly more secretive about how they conducted their business. Experts in "industrial espionage" were hired to keep the left hand from knowing what the right hand was doing, while the public remained completely unaware of the workings of either. A perfect example of the new corporate secrecy has been the relationship between industry and the environment. Over the last half-century, the dumping of waste and toxic leakage from manufacturing and processing plants has become shrouded in a smoke screen of half-truths, deceptions, and outright lies on the part of corporations fearing environmental responsibility, either enforced or volunteered, would cut too deeply into profit margins.

From poisoned rivers to exploitative drug companies to fraud at the savings and loan to child labor in the international garment industry, a cynicism of cover-up, spin control, and disinformation under the guise of public relations has become part of the contemporary art of doing business.

Maybe the only thing that consistently saves us from some Orwellian totalitarianism, complete with the Thought Police and the Ministry of Truth we met in *1984,* is that human beings not only want to know, but when gathered in groups, are also almost incapable of keeping secrets. Through the years, it has been the whistle blowers, the leakers of facts, the courageous individuals who have risked their jobs, their liberty, and sometimes their actual lives to stand up and say "enough already" who have given us at least some idea of what was really going on and what was being done to us under the dark cloak of secrecy. A Karen Silkwood may not exist in every industrial plant that threatens the workers' health or endangers the surrounding environment, but thankfully there have been enough agitators and iconoclasts to damn the consequences and give us at least a part of the picture. We may not be able to see the forest for the trees, but at least we are aware we're in a forest.

Unfortunately, a lot of the time a forest can be a dark, deceptive, and scary place. Unknown things rustle in the undergrowth or in the leaves overhead, and patterns of shadows can play on the imagination. When people are deprived of the truth, they settle for rumor, scuttlebutt, speculation, and out-and-out fiction. In times of stress, the need to have at least the illusion of knowing can outstrip even obvious implausibility. A military unit facing combat is the perfect model. The more the lowly grunts are kept in the dark, the more the rumors flourish and the grapevine hums. Someone has always heard something on the QT, and someone else is always absolutely certain what damn-fool plans the generals are cooking up. One way or another, the information vacuum will be filled even if it's with total fabrication.

In addition to wanting to know and not being good at keeping secrets, folks also like to boast. To be in the know when everyone else is baffled gives one an edge over the rest, and in this age of mass communication, to claim to be in the know is also to have a shot at a marketable product. In the days of sailing ships, old mariners scored shots of rum and mugs of ale by telling tales of monsters and mermaids to gullible landlubbers. Today, individuals who claim they once worked in secret government facilities with parts of flying saucers will fascinate the paying customers at UFO conventions with tales of aliens and high conspiracies. They will write books, establish Web sites, appear on TV, and peddle movie scripts in Hollywood. The late William Burroughs called it "the Chicken Little industry"—of which this book is shamelessly a part—noting that there was always a buck to make out of predicting the end of the world or revealing the inside dope on conspiracies in the corridors of power. Put the two together and you even have a long-running hit TV series like *The X-Files*.

The reality may be that all too many of us actually prefer to believe the fantastic over the mundane. Maybe the sky is falling, but isn't life also a bit more romantic with the nervous thrill that maybe the end really is at hand? And even if the sky isn't falling, aren't the nights more exciting with beings from other worlds buzzing around in them? These are exciting times for those who believe themselves to be living in the biblical "End Times," shortly to be called to do Apocalyptic battle with the forces of Satan. On a whole other level, a national poll reveals that some 70 percent of Americans do not believe that Lee Harvey Oswald was the lone gunman in the assassination of President John F. Kennedy. What the pollsters didn't ask was whether those 70 percent of Americans felt better believing that their president was killed by an elaborate conspiracy than by some isolated nut with a mail-order rifle and a head full of sour politics. If the lone nut could get the president, didn't that make life so random that anything could supposedly happen to anyone at any time? In the traumatic wake of the JFK assassination and the subsequent murders of Malcolm X, Martin Luther King, and Robert Kennedy, the concept of conspiracy offered a certain degree of chilly comfort. At least it possessed sufficiently evil stature to explain the pain.

One thing should not be forgotten, however. Even though the existence of a conspiracy may be what a lot of people want, both psychologically and emotionally, to believe for their own needs, it does not mean that their instincts are wrong and by no means indicates that a conspiracy doesn't exist.

While many people may accept any explanation rather than none, the U.S. government, over the past half-century, has not been particularly good at—or forthcoming with—explanations of what it's up to. As a body politic, however, it is also not terribly good at lying—even though the body should be well practiced in the art, having often lied throughout its more than two hundred years of life, right out to the very boundaries of the Constitution. On too many occasions, those in authority appear to adopt an attitude of disdainful contempt for the ones to whom they are supposed to answer. Far too many of our leaders take it as written that the mass of the population is both stupid and gullible. Okay, so en masse, men and women may not act overly smart, but we do seem possessed of a fairly reliable gut instinct that tells us when we're seriously being sold a bill of goods. To see this instinct in action, one has to look no further than the report of the Warren Commission on the assassination of JFK.

The great mistake of the Warren Commission may have been that it expected to be believed in the first place. Its unilateral creation of a case against Lee Harvey Oswald as the lone gunman shamelessly ignored any facts that failed to fit the thesis. It relied so heavily on clearly preposterous scenarios like Arlen Specter's "magic bullet" theory that one could assume it was only interested in having an explanation—any explanation—in place as quickly as possible, and truth was very low on the list of priorities. Or perhaps Lyndon Johnson didn't give a damn whether his Warren Report was believed or not. If nothing else, it bought him precious time. In the most charitable context, Johnson could well have been entering the investigation with a very real fear of what might be found. A Soviet or Castro-Cuban connection could bring the world to the edge of nuclear war. The revelation of a major domestic conspiracy could collapse the entire structure of national government. Facing the prospects of doomsday or anarchy, the tactical need was for a breathing space to take whatever action was warranted, away from the glare of the media. If the flimsy lone gunman cover story held up long enough to quietly negotiate with the Russians because some crew of rogue KGB spooks decided to take out the U.S. president, then all is well and good. If it stayed in place while domestic conspirators were neutralized, equally fine.

In a less kindly light, Johnson could have been going into the JFK investigation knowing exactly what the story was, either because he was part of the plot himself—he was, after all, as Oliver Stone reminded us, the primary beneficiary of Kennedy's death—or because J. Edgar Hoover laid out the details of the conspiracy almost as soon as the shooting stopped. In this grim scenario, the time bought by the Warren Report was even more crucial, and the implausibility was a definite asset. Any real JFK murder investigation might instantly be overrun with amateur investigators, conspiracy theorists, and time-wasting crazies. If anyone like New Orleans DA Jim Garrison made any serious attempt to sift the real facts, he could be dismissed along with the paranoids and the nuts. The world would enter an era of conflict and debate, analysis and counter-analysis—"a looking-glass world, people"—and it might take thirty years or more to match all the pieces of the jigsaw. By that time, the majority of the players would be dead and gone. Meanwhile, the real objective had been achieved. The uncontrollable Kennedy was off the bridge, and the ship of state was full ahead all engines for the Vietnam War and a military industrial bonanza.

Fortunately, it didn't happen that way. The conspiracy buffs, looking to spot gunmen on the grassy knoll in blurry photographs, turned over a great many unrelated but highly embarrassing stones. They unearthed Operation Mongoose and the CIA plots to kill Fidel Castro. The revelations of the CIA's history of experiments with LSD, brainwashing, and mind control—which would ultimately lead to the investigations by the 1976 Rockefeller Commission—were largely a result of probes into the background and CIA ties of Lee Harvey Oswald. More importantly, after the Kennedy assassination, something very radical happened to the state of paranoia in the Free World. It was taken out of the hands of politicians and given back to the people.

During the sub-zero Cold War of the 1950s, paranoia was completely controlled by the state. Fallout shelters and "duck and cover" atomic attack drills, HUAC and Joe McCarthy, the imprisonment of the Hollywood Ten, and the execution of Julius and Ethel Rosenburg (guilty or innocent) all manipulated public anxiety and clearly sent the message that the only thing to fear after communism was the government itself. When the shots rang out in Dealey Plaza and, within minutes, fingers were pointing at Oswald and no one else, all trust in politicians died right along with JFK. Without a blind belief that those in power knew best, manipulation became impossible. People not only demanded their own sources of information but began to create them. The alternative press that emerged in the 1960s—but still exists today albeit in a far mellower, less strident, and more commercial form—provided a spur to the more mainstream media to act as a watchdog on the covert maneuvers of the intelligence community, to monitor the wheelings, dealings, and cover-ups of those in authority, and to challenge and debate the government line on everything from recreational drugs to AIDS. In an almost organic consensus, people wanted to know in the worst way—if only to prevent another Warren Commission from treating them like idiots. It could be said that this wanting to know, and the fact that the *Washington Post* was willing to tell them, was really what stopped Richard Nixon from getting away scot-free after Watergate.

If the Warren Commission overestimated the public gullibility with regard to the Kennedy Assassination, then the U.S. Air Force's Project Grudge and Bluebook managed to insult the intelligence of the U.S. people in the matter of UFOs. When, from 1947 onward, large numbers of strange-moving lights started to appear in the sky and were dubbed "unidentified flying objects" or "flying saucers," the Air Force's best effort was condescendingly glib press releases that identified the things as weather balloons, marsh gas, oddly shaped clouds, flocks of migrating birds, and the planet Venus. Everyone who watched TV or read the newspapers and news magazines knew that these lights in the sky had been observed not just by drunks, teenagers, and Verne and Bubba fishing in the swamp, but by trained observers: cops, air traffic controllers, and military and civilian aircrews. These were all people who could tell birds and Venus from some weird radar blips zigzagging over Lubbock, Texas, in formation or buzzing Washington, D.C., in large numbers.

Again, the public was thrown back on its own paranoid resources. When the military fobbed folks off with marsh gas, the way was opened for all manner of less-official explanations. One of the first into the UFO information vacuum was a character called George Adamski, who lived on the slopes of Mt. Palomar in Southern California. He announced in his book *Flying Saucers Have Landed* that not only had he seen the UFOs in the sky, but one had landed near his house. He had taken photographs, and held conversations with the craft's occupants, who had taken him for a ride in the spaceship. By the time Adamski reached the point of describing romantic encounters with beautiful, blonde Venusians, the pu pretty much lost confidence in him, but his basic premise still stuc ing any other acceptable explanation, extraterrestrial spacecraft ma much sense as anything else. The idea would flourish and grow, clear -p to the present day, gathering a massive and convoluted weight of informational baggage along the passage of time.

Much like Lyndon Johnson and the Warren Commission, the Air Force officers assigned to the UFO investigation may well have suffered some trepidation about what they might find. The possibilities that these things were radical Nazi aircraft from the end of World War II or equally radical Soviet weapons were hardly a happy prospect. The third option, that the flying objects really were not of this Earth, took the Air Force into even more dangerous territory. Just like the Warren Commission, they may have simply fed the public any line of garbage while they attempted to find out what the things really were. Again, it's also possible that the Air Force knew exactly what the UFOs were, either because they were some secret U.S. project or because after the alleged Roswell crash or another similar incident they had ample evidence that the things were extraterrestrial craft and imposed the tightest security clampdown while wondering how to break the news to the rest of the world without creating massive social, cultural, and religious upheavals.

The motives of George Adamski are a lot easier to guess at and almost certainly involved three possible choices. The first was that he simply exploited the flying saucer furor with stories that were lies from start to finish, that his films and photographs were fakes, and that he was nothing more than an unscrupulous showman profiting from a media fad and the information void created by a condescending military. The second—being charitable again—was that Adamski really did undergo some kind of experience that set his money-making sideshow in motion, but after the initial story was told and maybe embroidered, the temptation was to go on churning out increasingly fantastic fabrications for the paying customers. The third was, of course, that he believed every word he said but was delusional and stone crazy.

In many respects, John Mack is the antithesis of George Adamski. Mack, a professor of psychiatry at Harvard Medical School who won a

Pulitzer Prize for a psychological biography of Lawrence of Arabia, became fascinated by the fact that by the start of the 1990s, up to a million Americans believed that at some point in their lives they had suffered abduction by aliens. As far as Mack was concerned, this kind of number indicated one of two things. Either a very large number of people were suffering from an almost identical psychotic delusion, or they really were being abducted by aliens—maybe not everyone who claimed to have been snatched by small, grey humanoids, but still significantly large numbers to warrant some kind of serious investigation. Logically, it should have been a job for either the military, the FBI, or the Centers for Disease Control, but none of these agencies appeared in any way interested so Mack decided to do it himself. Almost from the moment that he began to examine the abduction phenomenon, Mack ran into a firestorm of academic hostility, criticism, and contempt. He was likened to Timothy Leary who, years earlier, had become notorious for his LSD experiments while at Harvard, and arguably threw his career away by pandering to what was nothing more than tabloid nonsense.

The abuse became even worse when, during the course of his research, Mack began to actually believe that in some of the cases he was studying, real abductions had taken place. Many of his colleagues derisively pointed out that the kind of hypnotic regression Mack used to help subjects recall the "missing time" during which they were aboard alien craft was prone to what was known as "false memory syndrome." Patients are conditioned—either consciously or unconsciously—to produce answers the therapist is seeking. Hypnotic regression therapy has also been extensively used in cases of repressed memories of child abuse and molestation, and infant exposure to Satanic cults. In these areas, imposed false memories have proved to be so major a problem that many doctors—and also lawyers in child custody and similar suits—have ceased to regard it as trustworthy.

Whatever the truth about George Adamski, John Mack, or any of the dozens of other UFO pundits who have come to the fore in the last four decades, it has absolutely no bearing on the real truth about those things in the sky. Adamski may have been lying or deranged, and Mack may be dealing in false memories or a collective psychosis. Until a fully authenticated alien appears on CNN, UFOs can be anything from a figment of the Jungian collective unconsciousness to the first scouts of an invasion force that plans to burn this planet to green glass with its rayguns. We are wholly, totally free to believe what we like—without the Air Force or any UFO buff having any say in the matter. We can even chose between needing to know and wanting to believe.

The problem with being in charge of our own paranoia rather than having some paternalist authority tell us what we should be thinking is that we must make our own choices, and here, on the threshold of the new millennium, the choices are far from few. Since the narrow secrecy of the Cold War 1950s, our sources of information have multiplied by quantum leaps. When Al Gore coined the phrase "the information superhighway," he almost certainly envisioned something streamlined, orderly, and neatly organized, and not the roaring anarchic dragstrip that it has grown into today, complete with cyber-hot rodders, galactic hitchhikers, and such a thundering rush of limitless data—true and false, profound and ludicrous—that sometimes it's hard to avoid being roadkill in the cultural overload. Where once we only had *Time*, *Life*, and *Newsweek*, a well-stocked newsstand can now stretch for nearly half a city block with specialist magazines on every conceivable subject from astrology to automatic weapons. Cable and satellite TV offer close to a hundred channels, and even the most rapid remote grazing can hardly keep up with even a fraction of the output. On the Internet, it is possible to move from Noam Chomsky to Marilyn Manson with a click of the mouse.

At one time, the jigsaw pieces with which we assembled our perception of the world had to be ferreted out one by one. We now live in a noisy marketplace where millions of bits of data, on even more millions of subjects, all jostle and vie for our attention, our trust, and our gullibility. An open market may represent the freedom to which we all aspire, but it can also be a raw, dirty, and sometimes dangerous place with its whores and con artists, its snakeoil salesmen, pickpockets, and false prophets. Everyone has either a secret agenda or the secret of an agenda, and a free market in information doesn't mean we are fundamentally any closer to the truth. Those in power still want to keep their secrets, but instead of merely brushing us off with a Warren Commission report or a Project Bluebook, the lies and disinformation become more flamboyant and seductive. Truth—real objective truth—is turned into a shell game of now you see it, now you don't.

The Gulf War may have been the greatest example so far of the new face of public deception. Although, through its brief duration, it was the most televised war in history, with CNN reporters actually inside the enemy capital, George Bush and his generals remembered the lesson of Vietnam. They went into Operation Desert Storm with an implacable determination that the people would see nothing that would turn them off or alienate their support. The news coverage was of a video game war, a seamless, micro-managed panorama of smart bombs, surgical strikes, stealth fighters, and battle tanks rolling forward, unopposed, past ranks of surrendering Iraqis. Even the eerie green, night-vision shots of the high-tech fireworks over Baghdad were so science fiction in their imagery that it was almost impossible to connect them with the reality that they were blowing up not only buildings and military installations, but also men, women, and children. The conventionally horrific images of the red fire and black smoke from the burning oil fields came after the shooting was over and Saddam Hussein's contempt for the environment needed to be underlined. Only much later did we begin to learn of the dark side of the war, of civilian casualties, of Gulf War Syndrome, of chemical weapons, and shells jacketed with spent uranium.

Without getting into psychiatric technicalities, the pop definitions of paranoia are numerous and often closer to the money than the shrinks like to admit. "Just because you're paranoid, it doesn't mean they ain't out to get you." "The light at the end of the tunnel is an oncoming train." On a more thoughtful level of cliché, "Paranoia is one way of making sense of the nonsensical." These definitions attempt an explanation, no matter how spurious, of a world that seems too complicated to be understood and far beyond any individual control. Even though Mulder's combined maxim dictates, "the truth is out there, but trust no one," the danger is in going too far with the assumption that we are consistently and constantly subject to a conspiracy of deception and manipulation. The temptation is to look for a unifying factor, a way in which one person, one group, or one thing is responsible for all that makes the modern world so chaotic and potentially frightening.

In the last few years, the term "Octopus Theory" has been bounced around not only in the world of secrets and hidden agendas but also in the psychiatric community. In essence, the Octopus Theory is the unifying factor taken to the ultimate extreme, the belief that everything in the world is the result of one vast and complicated conspiracy. The rational person will dismiss the idea, and the shrink will warn you not to go there, it leads to either fascism or conversations with an invisible friend. Shrink and rationalist will agree that anything like the Octopus Theory is simply too easy, too neat a paranoid shortcut to a false solution.

On the other hand, just as most other states of mind, both rational and irrational, cannot be separated from the surrounding culture, paranoia has always drawn directly on the immediate cultural ground clutter. This is nowhere more noticeable than when individual paranoia erupts into deadly violence. When, in the rock 'n' roll 50s, Charles Starkweather and his girlfriend, Caril Fugate, went on their Nebraska badlands killing spree, his self-promoted image as a combination of James Dean and the Angel of Death fitted perfectly with the contemporary concept of the "crazy, mixed-up kid," and as such, he became, in some quarters, a homicidal teen folk hero. In the same way, a decade and a half later, the Manson Family, with their quasi-Satanism and apocalyptic doctrine of Helter Skelter gleaned from a weird amalgam of The Book of Revelation and The Beatles' White Album, represented the dark side of 60s flower power. Serial killer Ted Bundy provided an obvious analog for the contradictions of the 70s "Me Generation" and the yuppies of the Reagan era, as almost like some monstrous comic book super-villain, he presented the daytime face of a charming and upwardly mobile young Republican, but in the interior darkness of his soul, he altered his ego to become the sexual stalker and slaughterer of attractive young women.

In the even more confused and media-inundated 90s, it became hard to truly assess whether Eric Harris and Dylan Klebold—the members of the Trenchcoat Mafia who attempted to blow away their entire high school, or at the very least, kill as many of their teachers and fellow students as they could before killing themselves—should be viewed as culturally created monsters or as a new manner of victim for whom the world had become their very own and highly delusional Octopus. Faced with the feeling that they had become terminal outsiders, the subjects of real or imagined prejudice, and an immediate environment that seemed to be nothing more than a perpetual conspiracy of insult and harassment, their reaction was to retreat into a personal fantasy world cut from whole-paranoid cloth, to look for comfort in threatening costumes, in an "us against them" defiant camaraderie of shock tactics, and in a kind of cybernetic virtual-mysticism in which death is presented as either irrelevant, negatable, or even a hoped-for release.

The Trenchcoat Mafia deliberately combined all of their favorite parts of the dark side of paranoid pop culture—movies like *The Matrix* and *The Crow,* video games like *Doom,* death metal rock 'n' roll, the outer limits of the Internet, mail-order *Soldier of Fortune* militia literature—to create a never-never land in which they were implacable and invincible heroes who could proudly proclaim "stay alive, stay different, stay crazy." This self-made universe served first as a refuge, then as an emotional boot camp in which to hone their paranoid rage, and finally, in the case of Harris and Klebold, as a base from which they could mount their suicide attack on the microcosm high school reality that had tormented them. In this they managed to turn the Octopus Theory on its head, and the two lone gunmen actually challenged reality with their lives.

As with Harris and Klebold, too much of our information comes to us via print or electronic media, both of which are frequently solitary vices devoid of healthy debate and discussion, and in our isolation we succumb to the temptation of seeing patterns where none exist—the post-industrial equivalent of making pictures in the fire. We learn that mutant frogs are growing extra legs in Minnesota, that a black market may exist in ex-Soviet nuclear weapons parts, that heavily armed guys in camouflage are running around the woods firmly convinced that troops of the New World Order in black helicopters are about to take over the country. It may be tempting to try and link them all, but no demonstrable relationship exists except that they are all happening in the same world at the same time, and they are all the products of varying degrees of human greed, fear, and stupidity.

Yet, just as we overcome the temptation to embrace the Octopus and decide that the modern world is not the product of some vast, all encompassing plot designed and ordered by a secret elite and its minions, but just a mess of random chances, one or another of these disturbing synchronous little loops show up just to keep us on edge. A New York City bum talks to Stuttering John on *The Howard Stern Show*, babbling how the Central Intelligence Agency planted microchips in his head to control and confuse his thinking. A harmless psycho? Maybe, until it starts to emerge that the operation he's raving about and the symptoms he's manifesting are uncomfortably close to those resulting from some of the CIA's MKULTRA mind control experiments as described by author John Marks in his 1979 book *The Search for the Manchurian Candidate*. As conservative scientists state confidently that no real evidence can be offered for global warming, half of Borneo catches fire live on CNN, and you can't help but wonder. Perhaps one of the oddest of these loops occurred at the same time as rational individuals, both lay and professional, were presenting a convincing case that the Octopus Theory is nothing more than a dangerous state of mind. James Ridgeway and David Vaughn of the *Village Voice* were digging into the 1991 death of journalist Danny Casolaro, who was writing a book on what he firmly believed was the real Octopus Conspiracy. Although his death was ruled a suicide, many close to Casolaro were not satisfied with the verdict, particularly when all his notes and manuscripts vanished and two strange national security-looking types even showed up at his funeral.

Thus, if for no other reason than to avoid the sudden and mysterious demise of anyone connected with the publication of this book, no theories are presented or conspiracies speculated upon here. Just the facts, ma'am, as Joe Friday used to say on *Dragnet*...along with the secrets, the lies, the small horrors, and the big rumors. All the mutant frogs, the alien invasion plans, and the hidden plots of government that can be crammed into the allotted pages. We don't even suggest that every word is the gospel truth, although every entry has at some time been presented as gospel. What the reader believes or disbelieves is entirely up to her or him. All we can do is offer the following pledge:

The Pledge—All of the entries included in this book have appeared in print, on the Internet, on TV, or have been repeated in authenticated conversation. The more transparent fabrications of the *Globe* or *Weekend World News* will not be included.

Key

To assist you in targeting the subject matter of the conspiracies, lies, and secrets contained in this book, each has been assigned one or more of the icons on this page. Moreover, boldface items in the text direct you to other entries.

Aliens

Assassination

Computers

Cults/Religion

Drugs

The Earth

End of the World

The Feds

Magnetism

Medicine

Nazis

Nuclear Power

Secret Societies

UFOs

None of the above

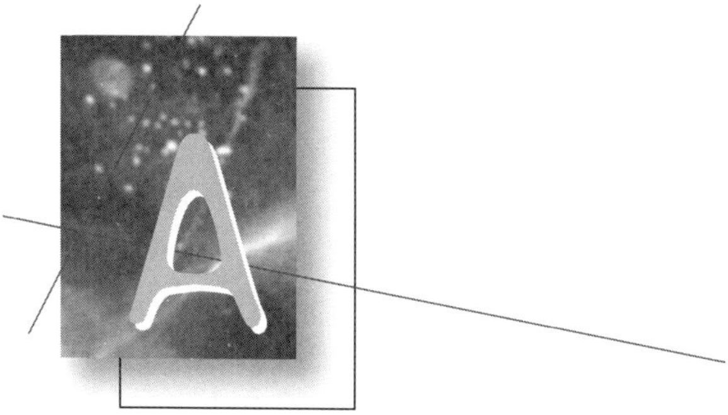

Abduction by Aliens

According to a survey of nearly 6,000 Americans conducted by the Roper organization between July and September of 1991, some hundreds of thousands, at the very least—and maybe as many as a million or more—U.S. citizens firmly believe that they have been abducted by alien beings on at least one occasion. Since that time, what amounts to a whole industry has formed around the phenomenon. Psychologists offer treatment to individuals who believe they may have been abducted. Computer tests have been designed to discover if we've been abducted without our knowledge, and academics like Harvard Medical School psychiatry professor Dr. John Mack have put their reputations on the line by jumping on the abduction book publishing bandwagon—in Mack's case, with the bestseller *Abduction*. In a sinister sidebar to the abduction claims, a number of conspiracy theorists are now claiming that alien abduction is a bizarre hoax, a cover for ultra-secret human experimentation by the **CIA** and other government agencies.

Acid Rain

Acid rain is still with us. Indeed, it is possibly more widespread than it was when it was one of the main concerns of environmentalists during the 1960s and 1970s and received maximum media coverage. Lately, one might be forgiven for thinking that acid rain had gone away, as it hardly seems to be mentioned either in the press or on television. An unfortunate side effect of the increased environmental awareness is the way in which both the media and the public almost faddishly fix on one particular symptom of environmental damage and tend to ignore those that have gone before. Attempts have been made in Europe and North America to reduce the levels of industrial pollutants that combine with rainfall to produce weak but relentless solutions of nitric, hydrochloric, and sulfuric acids. But these controls didn't start to have any noticeable effect until large areas of woodland like Germany's Black Forest had all but been destroyed.

Today, the worst acid rain threat comes from the newly industrialized emergent nations and the ecological chaos in the former Soviet Union. Also China, as it moves into a quasi-capitalist twenty-first century, appears bent on repeating all the environmental outrages that Europe and America are only just slowly beginning to bring under control. So, while we worry about global warming, the disruption of the weather system, the melting icecaps, and the destruction of the rain forests, give a thought to acid rain. It is still killing forests as efficiently as the graders, bulldozers, chainsaws, and backhoes that are ripping their way into Borneo and the Amazon.

Adamski, George

By one set of somewhat benign and uncritical criteria, George Adamski was the first human being to be contacted by aliens in the post World War II period of the worldwide "flying saucer" craze. According to a less generous judgement, he was the first huckster to get into the UFO racket on an international, pop culture, mass level. In his books, *Flying Saucers Have*

Landed (1953) and *Inside the Space Ships* (1956), Adamski made the fairly astonishing claim that at his California home on the slopes of Mt. Palomar, he had seen strange objects in the skies—as many others claimed at the time. He claimed that these objects had actually landed, revealing themselves to be spacecraft from Venus and other planets in the solar system. He had conducted lengthy conversations with the craft's occupants, and had a romantic tryst with a beautiful, female Venusian who warned him, in rather general and obvious terms, that if mankind didn't abandon its nuclear weapons programs and start treating its planet with a bit more care and kindness, the consequences could be terminally dire. These revelations made Adamski an instant and sought-after celebrity and, at the peak of his fame, he was even accorded a private audience with the Pope.

Unfortunately, much of Adamski's former life did little to enhance his credibility. He immigrated to the U.S. from Poland in the 1930s and attempted to set up shop as one of the thousands of gurus and teachers of universal mystic truths in Southern California. His philosophy seems to have been a fairly unoriginal, pre-hippie blend of various Eastern religions, and when the guru business didn't pay too well, he also worked as a handyman in a roadside diner. It didn't help his credibility that his aliens were tall and stunningly handsome, Nordic humanoids who greatly resembled a Swedish heavy metal band dressed in jogging suits. Many of Adamski's early critics found it hard to accept the Eurocentricity of these Venusians. They seemed just too much of a Hitlerian ideal for many to swallow with any ease.

Another area in which Adamski came under immediate fire was for his alleged photographs of the alien craft. His books were profusely illustrated with his own grainy shots of the small disc-shaped scout craft and the big cylindrical mothership. One researcher even went so far as to produce a commercial chicken brooder used by farmers to warm newly-hatched chicks. The disc-shaped chicken brooder, readily available from a well-known agricultural mail-order catalog, conformed exactly with Adamski's scout ship. The real downfall of George Adamski and his claims of close encounters, however, came when the space program got under way and probes sent to Venus proved conclusively that the planet was too hot and had too violent a weather system to support a population of tall, Nordic demigods.

George Adamski died of a heart attack, penniless in 1965. He did, however, leave one odd legacy. Chicken brooders notwithstanding, variations on the Adamski "scout ship"—the one that resembles an inverted soup plate with a small turret mounted on top and supported from beneath by three large hemispheres that are supposed to be part of the propulsion unit—has become virtually the generic flying saucer. It has appeared in movies, comic books, science fiction illustrations, and even plastic construction kits.

Addison's Disease

Writer and wit Gore Vidal puts a whole new spin on the **assassination of JFK** by making the suggestion, in his 1997 memoir *Palimpsest*, that although a closely-guarded secret, President John F. Kennedy suffered from Addison's Disease, a debilitating and often fatal malfunction of the adrenal gland, and would not have lived very much longer had the fatal shooting in Dallas not occurred.

Air America

The **Central Intelligence Agency**'s very own airline. Although Air America operated in Laos, Cambodia, and Vietnam from around 1967 to 1975, similar quasi-civil aviation operations have been staged in other areas of intense intelligence-community activity. One of the more recent examples to surface was when Colonel Oliver North—now a radio talk show host—was running guns to the anti-communist, Nicaraguan Contras during the Iran-Contra phase of the **Reagan** administration. Because the "private" airline involved was operating on a commercial and highly cost-effective basis, it was deemed ludicrous that the planes should return to the U.S. with empty cargo holds. Thus, a deal was struck with the Cali cartel of Colombian cocaine exporters to provide profitable return cargoes. The rule became guns south, cocaine north, and had the added advantage of assisting the Cali cartel in their power struggle with the Medellin cartel led by the more left-leaning Carlos Escobar.

The prototype for this kind of bizarre free enterprise was, of course, the trade in arms for drugs that took place between the CIA and Air America and the various anti-communist guerrilla groups fighting the Pathet Lao—the Laotian equivalent of the Vietcong—in the neighboring country of Laos. In the case of the Laotian anti-communists, many of them were also the country's largest opium producers, and their war with the Pathet Lao was less a matter of ideology than an attempt to protect their business interests and their poppy fields from the insurgents. Air America was used extensively to ferry in arms, ammunition, and CIA advisors to the Laotian anti-communists. Unfortunately, Air America found that, in return, it was flying out with the same people's raw opium that, after being refined in Thailand, found its way back to Saigon in the form of heroin and then went on sale to the grunts in the jungles and rice paddies. The guns for opium deal may have seemed expedient at the time in combating the Pathet Lao, but in the long run, it looked dangerously akin to the drunken cowboy who fires his gun into the air with little or no idea where the bullet may eventually land.

By the mid-1990s, the end of the Cold War against the Soviets, the great leaps made in spy satellite technology, plus a number of emerging scandals brought the CIA's role into serious question. It became the object of such congressional disdain that suggestions were circulated in the Washington corridors of power that the agency should be disbanded. The CIA, however, is more than capable of finding a use for both itself and its private airlines in the new millennium, and because we never find out about these things until after the fact, there's actually no knowing what they might be up to right now.

Airline Flu

How many people do you know who, immediately after a trip in a commercial airliner of four hours or more, come down with some annoying upper-respiratory complaint, some variation on what is coming to be known as "airline flu"? Commercial airliners seem to be progressively becoming airborne tanks of commingling bacteria. One person sneezes and everyone else gets sick. Part of the problem is that airlines, in these competitive and cost-conscious times, save considerable quantities of fuel by not recycling the air in their planes as much as they used to. The irony in all this is that in days gone by, before cigarette smoking was outlawed on all domestic and many overseas flights, the cabin air had to be almost constantly changed to vent the tobacco smoke. With no visible smoke, the air in the aircraft now looks cleaner, but seemingly, the germs have a field day. Did someone say you just can't win?

Alaska

In the summer of 1998, the *New York Times* reported just one more indication that the governments of the world perhaps should be taking the possible threat of global warming a little more seriously. The state of Alaska appears to be thawing out quite rapidly. Temperatures in the far north have risen significantly over the last thirty years. As the summers become warmer and the winters less cold, glaciers have begun to shrink and the permafrost is melting. Trees sink into the spongy ground and tilt over at strange angles, giving rise to what is becoming known as "the drunken forest effect." Scientists warn that this may only be the start of much more radical changes.

Alien Autopsy

Remember the film footage aired by the Fox Network in 1996 that purported to be of an autopsy on a dead extraterrestrial recovered from a crashed UFO; footage that created considerable controversy as to whether it was authentic or fake? One claim for its original discovery was that it was found in a U.S. Army film archive during a search for Army footage of **Elvis Presley** going about his duties as a draftee in Germany in the late 1950s.

This story circulated freely when the alien autopsy broadcast was first being promoted. Later, however, it quietly faded away.

Alpha Draconus

The home world in the Alpha Centuari of the sinister reptilian aliens who some believe are currently in cahoots with **The New World Order** to take over planet Earth.

Amish Cocaine Dealers

The Amish, descendants of a German Anabaptist sect that has maintained settlements in rural Pennsylvania since 1693, traditionally shun the comforts of the modern world, rejecting such twentieth-century inventions as TV, automobiles, and even zippers, all of which are regarded as "sins of pride." Thus it came as something of a shock when, in 1998, two young Amish, both named Abner Stolzfus but unrelated (not uncommon among the Amish), were charged with conspiracy to sell cocaine with a street value of more than $1 million.

Amphetamine

Wanna get real paranoid? Hear the electricity whispering in the wires and have the entire shadow world right there in the room with you? Try staying up for a number of days on the drug amphetamine, you may well experience all of that and more. Invented by Nazi chemists during World War II at the instigation of Luftwaffe chief Hermann Goering to keep his pilots alert and awake on long combat missions (and because Goering's personal supply of cocaine had been jeopardized by the shifting winds of war), the essential function of amphetamine is to block perceptions. The user is largely unaware of—or able to ignore—fatigue, hunger, and many normal physical inputs. The downside is that with the human psyche isolated from its usual responses and deprived of the normal flow of basic bodily information, it tends to rattle around loose in the consciousness, creating a frequently disturbed and paranoid fantasy perception.

Amphetamines became a common street drug during the 1960s and were largely condemned by the psychedelic counterculture as a "bad drug" due to the high levels of obsessive behavior, psychosis, and irrational violence observed among speed freaks. The graffito "speed kills" was daubed on walls from London to San Francisco.

In addition to Nazi airmen, other noted users included Jack Kennedy—who was reputed to have been shot up on a regular basis by **Dr. Max Jacobson** with a cocktail of speed and vitamin B12 during the tense days of the Cuban Missile Crisis. Johnny Cash and **Elvis Presley**—who learned from his mother that speed can help one keep one's weight under control when on a diet of hamburgers and ice cream—were also users. Speed was the fashion drug for models of the "Twiggy" era, London mods of the 1960s, transvestites of the Warhol scene, punks of the 1970s, various rock and roll bands, and long-haul truck drivers.

If it's any consolation, the speed now consumed in the U.S. is strictly an American drug. It can be cheaply manufactured from easily obtained agricultural chemicals—primarily the bulk ephedrine fed to chickens in intensive rearing units to prevent respiratory complaints. For a long time, the Hell's Angels motorcycle club controlled the speed trade in the U.S., but when many of the club's members were jailed under racketeering statutes, the business passed to anyone who could figure out the formula.

Anal Probe

A recurrent scatological appendage to **alien abduction** stories. In addition to quasi-medical unpleasantness like having filaments thrust up their noses and through the sinuses into the brain, or similar filaments pushed into their navels, many abductees—both male and female—also claim to have been subjected to the phallic and highly Freudian intrusion of the anal probe. Its purpose, of course, is known only to the aliens.

Annunaki

According to legend, the Sumerian civilization of 6,000 years ago was founded by visiting aliens called the Annunaki from the planet Niburu, the alleged twelfth planet in our solar system.

Antibiotics

A deep-seated but not too publicly-voiced fear in the medical/drug manufacturing complex is that antibiotics will soon become obsolete and totally ineffective as literally millions of strains of bacteria mutate themselves into immunity to penicillin and its life-saving cousins. In an explosive end-run around these conventional, taken-for-granted treatments, what are now considered minor domestic ailments could become serious and even life threatening as bacteria develop more resistance. Already, what were previously thought of as beaten diseases like tuberculosis are reasserting themselves. Part of the problem is that antibiotics are overused. Many low-income folks self-medicate with drugs leftover from previous ailments or with ones that were originally prescribed for family or friends. Antibiotics are all too frequently given for viral complaints to guard against possible opportunistic infections.

An early preview of what might happen occurred during the Vietnam War when various broad-spectrum antibiotics were given as prophylactics to prostitutes in Saigon and Manila, and strains of antibiotic-resistant sexually transmitted infections were created. Essentially, all we need for a full-blown global plague that would make the Black Death look like a head cold is one airborne, highly resistant, mutant bacteria.

Already, Japanese researchers have isolated a new strain of Staph Aureus—a common bacteria that infects cuts and scratches and is part of a microbiological undertow in most hospitals. The strain has taken on "superbug" status by becoming immune to all existing forms of antibiotics, including Vancomycin, currently considered the antibiotic of last resort. With more such superbugs inevitably just over the horizon, one might think that all efforts would be made to restrict unnecessary use of antibiotics. Sorry, think again. Bandaid has just come on the market with an over-the-counter, antibiotic adhesive plaster.

Antichrist, The

According to noted Southern Californian psychic Sean David Morton, the Antichrist is already among us, just biding his time until he reveals himself and begins to wreak global havoc. His name is unknown but is an anagram of the letters RAYPOZ. He is 5′ 10″, weighs 165 pounds, and was born in Bethlehem, Israel on February 5, 1962. He now holds either Iranian or Pakistani citizenship. He has no permanent address but travels between Syria, Jordan, Iran, London, and New York, staying in homes owned by seven of the world's wealthiest men. There would seem to be only one snag in all this. Morton, who charges up to $25 a ticket for his prophetic lectures, has been pushing this revelation of the Antichrist since the early 1990s. Originally, this embodiment of evil was going to make himself known to the world in 1994. Now his going public is up to 1999 and rising. He may even be hard pressed to emerge before the millennium.

On the other hand, an obscure Pentecostal sect operating out of a storefront on 173rd Street in New York continues to believe that Michael Jackson is the Antichrist.

Area 51

Only America has a phenomenon as peculiar as Area 51. Where else would one of the nation's most secret military bases—so secret, in fact, that the government wouldn't publicly admit that it actually exists—become a highly publicized tourist attraction? Australians don't gather to stare at **Pine Gap**, the highly secret communications center in the outback. The British don't hang out around their nuclear weapons establishments, unless of course they are part of a peace protest.

Area 51 is now such a major part of late twentieth-century mythology that it is almost impossible to separate fact from speculation and rumor. The facts are that a combination of the U.S. Air Force and Navy, and possibly a number of other agencies, operate a vast 38,500 acre military complex 150 miles north, northwest of Las Vegas near the small town of Rachel, Nevada, near the high desert ranges where atomic bombs were tested during the 1940s and 1950s. The area is heavily guarded by SWAT-style armed guards supplied by the private **Wackenhut** security corporation, something that may be of dubious legality on a military installation. For a number of years now, bright and erratically moving lights—some performing maneuvers that would be impossible for conventional aircraft flown by human pilots—have been seen regularly over the area. They have been repeatedly filmed and videotaped, and the tapes have aired on local TV news shows both in Las Vegas and Los Angeles, as well as on shows like *Sightings* and *Strange Universe*.

The spectacle of the lights in the sky is, of course, what attracts the tourists. At one time, they watched from an area of high ground known as Freedom Ridge, but then the military made a compulsory purchase of large tracts of land surrounding the base, and a clear view of Area 51 is now impossible. Debate continues over this purchase. On one level, many local residents challenge its legality, citing the fact that a number of ranchers have long-established grazing rights on the land. Tourists and UFOlogists want to know, because anything that might be going on inside the installation is clearly visible to Russian spy satellites, why the military should go to such lengths to prevent loyal U.S. citizens from knowing what they're doing. It has certainly been made abundantly clear that spectators are far from welcome. Land adjoining the base is riddled with motion sensors and other high-tech security devices, and anyone straying too close is chased, threatened, and even run off the road by the Wackenhunt guards.

The government will not acknowledge that Area 51 is even there, so we have no official story. Therefore, the only available information as to its purpose—and need for such absolute secrecy—is either a matter of conjecture, informed or otherwise, or the word of individuals like Robert Lazar who claim to have worked inside the facility. Lazar now produces videotapes and works the lecture circuit, informing all who will purchase a ticket that the true function of Area 51 is the testing of alien technology under the ultimate supervision of the shadowy oversight group known as **Majestic 12**.

The theories about what really goes on inside the place fall into three basic categories. The most conservative set of scenarios is that Area 51 is a much more elaborate extension of the old Nellis Test Range, the home of various black projects, including the entire gamut of radar-deceiving **stealth** technology, as well as the mystery-shrouded **Aurora** aircraft and a form of experimental external combustion propulsion unit known as the "**Pumpkin Seed**." The latter two are most likely to be the cause of the strange lights in the sky. The second class of theory includes all of the above plus the claim that the installation now houses all of the recovered debris from all the UFO crashes that occurred in the U.S. in the last half-century, and scientists are busy with the reverse engineering of what they have in an attempt to learn as much as they can about alien technology.

Lately, a number of experts have cast doubts on the whole idea of reverse engineering—the technique of attempting to learn the nature of a machine by analyzing fragments of its parts. They cast doubt on the idea that human beings can learn anything about a machine capable of crossing interstellar space. The alien technology needed to make such an incredible journey would be so advanced that we simply wouldn't know where to start. As one researcher put it, "it would be like giving Pythagoras, the Greek mathematician, a part of a video camera and expecting him to figure out television. He might be a genius, but he'd have no terms of reference within which to work."

The third and most extreme theory—and the one that probably brings the tourists to spend their money at the souvenir stands in Rachel and at the Little A'Le'Inn—at least manages to get around the problem of reverse engineering. This one claims that aliens themselves are in residence in Area 51, instructing human scientists in their technology and allowing human pilots to fly hybrid aircraft that incorporate both human and alien design factors. On a more sinister level, these aircraft may not be the only hybrids in the deal. According to many rumors, part of the aliens' end of the bargain is to be able, in the deep underground levels of the base, to conduct genetic experiments on human subjects with a possible goal of creating a human/alien hybrid being.

Recently, a new twist has turned up in the Area 51 story. Sometime in the early 1990s (accounts differ on the time) hostilities are said to have broken out between humans and aliens that led to a brief and decisive armed conflict in which the humans were forced to withdraw from the lower levels of Area 51 and leave the aliens in complete control. Similar stories have emerged about other alleged alien underground enclaves like the ones at Laguna Cartagena in Puerto Rico and Archuleta Mesa near Dulce, New Mexico. The story is that the deal with the ETs has now been renegotiated in their favor, and Area 51 and the other installations are now their turf with the prime human function being to keep other humans out. If any of this is believable, it would seem that the only conclusion to be drawn is that the aliens have now entered phase two of classic colonial infiltration. First they come bearing gifts, then they set up forts. The third phase is, of course, complete takeover.

Arkansas

The following story was reported by none other than Norman Mailer. In the early 1980s, the **Reagan** administration feared that Nicaraguan Sandinistas would destabilize Central America, turn it communist, and then invade Texas. Some bright young men at the **NSA** and the **CIA** decided that, clandestinely, they had to hold and totally control a small Third World country. They felt they needed such a place as a permanent covert weapon system test facility and a central base for black operations. Their problem was they couldn't come up with a nation with a sufficiently passive and docile indigenous population that could be relied on to remain compliant in perpetuity, particularly if CIA agents (Company spooks) were tearing up the landscape, mutilating cattle, and spraying the place with psychedelic nerve gas. Then an older hand interrupted. He told them, in effect, "Hell, boys, you won't find anywhere more Third World than the Arkansas backwoods, and it's right here in the U.S. of A. All you need is a smart, unscrupulous young governor to help you acquire the real estate. Of course, you might have to pay him off by helping him get to be president."

Army of the Dead

Since mid-1995, the rumor has been circulating in some of the more fearful sectors of the Internet that Islamic Fundamentalist agents are roaming northern and central Africa, recruiting an army of men who are either **HIV** positive or have full-blown AIDS. Initially, these doomed recruits would be used on suicide missions or as human bombs, much like the **Shaheed** killers currently directed by the Hamas terror group, happy to die in the service of Allah, and as warriors in the Jihad, be assured of their place in paradise. As the pandemic continues to spread however, this Army of the Dead will increase in size until it is able to mount full-scale "human wave" attacks and possibly commence "A Great March of Destruction" on South Africa, Israel, or even Europe.

Assassination of John F. Kennedy, The

The JFK assassination will simply not go away. It is not only a major turning point in the above-ground history of both the U.S. and the world but also provides the shadow watershed for most of our deepest and darkest paranoias. Obviously, the root of the morbid fascination that has now surrounded the assassination for the best part of four decades has to be the idea that "if they can get the president, they can get anyone," but that fatalistic resignation was only the start of the grim obsession. Although the academic debate over the personal and political record of John Fitzgerald Kennedy—both his accomplishments and his failures—will probably be continued for centuries to come, there can be no question that the Camelot era of the Kennedy administration was a time of unprecedented hope on the part of the American people. Hindsight may decree that hope was perhaps unfounded or over optimistic, but at the time, a handsome and charismatic leader living in the White House with his equally attractive wife and young family at least created the illusion that all things were possible.

The images of a smiling man, acknowledging the cheers of the crowd from the back of an open car in the fall Texas sunshine, struck down by a hail of bullets is seared into the minds of those who lived through that time and many who came after. In a handful of seconds, that unique hope of the early 1960s was destroyed for all time. At first, not only America but the entire world simply went through the process of denial, shock, and grief. It wasn't until two days after the assassination, when Jack Ruby shot Lee Harvey Oswald at point-blank range in the basement of Dallas police headquarters, that shock turned to anger and the sinking, if unfocused gut feeling that dark and hidden forces were at work in the death of the president. As subsequent events unfolded, and the stories and rumors began to circulate, the sinking feeling grew into a deep and troubled suspicion that agendas were at work that didn't in any way include the peace of the world or simple prosperity at home.

The Warren Commission, quickly convened by President Lyndon Johnson to allay public fears, only concerned itself with proving the guilt of Lee Harvey Oswald as the lone gunman, rather than conducting a thorough and unbiased investigation of the crime. Far from allaying fear, the obvious shortcoming of the Warren Commission only served to further convince the American people that they were being deceived regarding this crucial and traumatic piece of history. By the end of the 1960s, over 70 percent of the adults in the U.S. refused to accept the conclusions of the Warren Report. What might be called assassination folklore began to pile up until its sheer weight could not be dismissed as paranoid fantasy or pop fiction masquerading as fact. The mysterious deaths and disappearances of witnesses and others closely associated with the assassination and its aftermath, plus all of the other paradoxes and anomalies that would follow, added support to the perception that the true facts in the case were being deliberately concealed, perhaps for all time.

Through the 1970s, public pressure built to such a level that it simply couldn't be ignored. In a belated response, Congress convened the

Select Committee on Assassinations of the House of Representatives. In 1979, the commission issued a report that concluded President Kennedy had "probably" been assassinated by a conspiracy that involved at least one more assassin, who had "probably" been firing from the grassy knoll in Dealey Plaza as many witnesses have always maintained. As of today, however, the Justice Department has made no move to identify this "other gunman" or attempt to apprehend members of this possible conspiracy.

In fact, a workable hypothesis for a conspiracy as deemed possible by the House Committee appears to have emerged and involves the intelligence community, anti-Castro Cubans, and organized crime. Although different commentators put different emphasis on different pieces of evidence, then assign varying motivations to those supposedly responsible and disagree about a wealth of detail, a body of evidence has been amassed that at least points in a probable direction. This is not to say that everyone who has gone on TV and into print with sensational conspiracy allegations is an unbiased seeker of truth. Many have used the JFK murder as a means to self-aggrandizement and personal profit, and to feed deep-seated but unrelated paranoias. Out on the fringes of conspiracy obsession, there are, moreover, those who claim JFK was killed because he knew too much about the invading aliens or as a ritual pagan sacrifice by the **Bavarian Illuminati**.

At the other end of the scale, a mainly conservative "lone gunman lobby" continues to cling to the findings of the Warren Commission with great tenacity, as any conspiracy theorist holds on to his or her concept of who did it. When 1991 saw the release of Oliver Stone's movie *JFK*, right-wingers accused Stone of everything short of high treason when they discovered that the film—ostensibly an account of New Orleans DA Jim Garrison's unsuccessful prosecution of businessman and CIA operative Clay Shaw—all but pointed the finger at an actual *coup d'etat* by groups inside the intelligence community, the armament industry, and Lyndon Johnson.

A mirror-image controversy blew up in 1998 when right-wing pundit Gerald Pozner published a defense of the Warren Commission in his book *Case Closed: Lee Harvey Oswald and the Assassination of JFK*. This time, the assassination buffs were up in arms that anyone could expect the public to yet again swallow the supposedly discredited lone gunman analysis.

After thirty-five years, the controversy over the Kennedy assassination endures. The arguments swing backward and forward. The frustrating part—and the reason no closure seems possible—is that by now, most of us are aware we may never really know the whole truth about who exactly killed JFK, unless of course a conspirator actually delivers a deathbed confession in the hope of clearing his soul. And even then, he probably wouldn't be believed.

Asteroid XF11

After its discovery in 1997, Asteroid XF11 threw the world's scientific community into a full-scale panic. According to projections of the asteroid's orbit made by NASA at the Jet Propulsion Lab in Pasadena, California, it began to look as though XF11 was going to impact with the Earth sometime in the year 2028. With a rough diameter of some ten miles and a mass adding up to hundreds of millions of tons, such an impact would essentially be a holocaust of immense earthquakes, tidal waves, firestorms, and then a global pall of dust and smoke, creating an "asteroid winter" that could last for centuries. Humanity and most other species currently living on the planet would go the way of the dinosaur, leaving little more than simple plant life and maybe some small mammals and fish. In late 1998, however, the JPL revised its math and newer data indicates that XF11 will actually miss the Earth by some 600,000 miles, which sounds like a comfortable margin, except in astronomical terms 600,000 is less than a whisker.

Aum Shrinrikyo

Until the serin nerve gas attack on the Tokyo subway in March of 1995, few people outside of Japan had ever heard of Aum Shrinrikyo (literally the "true teaching of Aum"). After the death of twenty-five rush hour commuters from the gas—a third-generation development of the zyklon-B used in the Nazi deathcamps—and the hospitalization of hundreds more, world media suddenly focused on the previously obscure sect that preached a blend of Buddhism and Christianity. The world wanted every grim detail, and what emerged appeared to be a high-tech version of the Manson Family. The difference was that Charlie's hippie mindbending had been replaced with seemingly unlimited capital, Japanese corporate-style efficiency, and full religious tax exemption. Aum still maintained the use of LSD and other drugs for mind alteration and the reprogramming of belief systems, and they seemed to have even taken the Manson concept of Helter Skelter mass slaughter to a brand new refined and streamlined level of horror. Where Charlie and his maidens of death only had knives, forks, and a few handguns, the Aum sect and its near-blind leader, Shoko Asahara, had at their disposal state-of-the-art terrorist weapons and easily concealable weapons of mass destruction.

When, in the wake of the subway attack, police broke into the Aum headquarters near the small village of Kamikuishiki on the lower slopes of Mt. Fuji, they discovered that the windowless, factory-like complex housed sophisticated chemical weapon labs and machine shops capable of turning out AK-47 assault rifles. Out back were even a helipad and a Soviet made MI-17 helicopter. Most sinister of all, the complex was equipped with industrial-strength microwave ovens capable of reducing human corpses to powder. Police estimated that more than thirty people had been executed in the Aum HQ for various infractions, while Aum members at the complex wore helmets equipped with antennae that were supposed to be constantly tuned to the thought waves of their leader.

Like so many other cults, the Aum started out as fairly benign. It appealed mainly to the young, and many of its recruiting pitches owed a great deal to Japanese comic books and TV cartoons—*manga* and *anime*—in which respect it bore a certain kinship to the **Heaven's Gate** sect. One of Asahara's major points was that, as in the cartoons and comics, youth would save the world—"the young warriors of truth." In 1990, with an estimated 50,000 members and more than a billion dollars in assets, Asahara decided the time was right to sweep to elected power in that year's

Japanese parliamentary elections. Sadly, the bid for office turned out to be an exercise not only in futility, but in total failure, with Asahara personally gleaning less than 2,000 votes. After the election debacle, attitudes seem to have rapidly changed.

Prior to 1990, Asahara had expected to be popularly proclaimed the new Buddha. After that time, he took a bleaker theological view, embracing Christian concepts like the Final Judgement and the ultimate battle of Armageddon, and a new-found hatred of Jews and **Freemasons**, even though neither group exist in Japan in anything but the smallest numbers. He also developed a fascination with the work of Serbian inventor and genius **Nikola Tesla**. Despite its grim outlook, however, the Aum sect continued to grow, amassing followers in both Russia and Australia. An Aum expedition even went into plague-stricken Zaïre, ostensibly to give aid, but seemingly, also to bring back samples of the ebola virus. The 1995 Kobe earthquake seems to have been the sign for which Asahara was waiting. Other mass murder attacks were planned to follow the subway outrage, but fortunately, Asahara and the core of the sect were quickly arrested. This is not to say that other members of Aum Shrinrikyo are not out there, waiting and biding their time.

Aurora

According to various leakages from that strange place where the ideas of aviation buffs, UFO theorists, and secret government paranoids all coincide, Aurora seems to be the code name for the ultra-secret, hypersonic, new spy plane that has replaced the now outdated Lockheed SR-71 Blackbird. The Aurora, with an alleged flight capability of up to ten times the speed of sound, is little short of a spaceship. It has an advantage over spy satellites—the orbits of which are easily plotted and predicted—in that it can inspect an area of the globe in minute detail without any advanced warning. No pictures of the Aurora have ever been released, but the scuttlebutt is that it's black (in every sense of the word), very large, and operates out of **Area 51** at Groom Lake, Nevada. Its test flights over Nevada and Southern California may also be responsible for some of the Area 51 UFO claims.

B

Baalbek

Although by no means as well known as the Great Pyramid, the ruins of Baalbek may be an even more impossible feat of ancient engineering than the mighty construction at Giza. Over the last thirty years the Baalbek site has been largely neglected due to its location in Lebanon's Bekaa Valley, the troubled war zone on the border with Israel. As with the pyramids and Stonehenge in England, conventional archeologists claim that Baalbek was constructed using ropes, rollers, and a whole lot of sweating workers, even though the average stone in the Trilithon structure weighs 800 tons and the largest as much as 1,000. Dissatisfied with this explanation, author and researcher Alan F. Alford contacted the British crane hire firm Baldwins Industrial Services and asked them how they would move the great Baalbek stones. Their experts suggested either a 1,000-ton capacity crane fitted with crawler tracks or a series of modular hydraulic trailers. In both cases, one of the major problems would be advance preparation of the ground over which the stones would have to be moved. Without solid roads under them, loads of that weight would simply cause the machine that was carrying them to sink into the ground. Oddly, no remains of this kind of construction roadway are detectable at the site. Baldwins experts, however, considered ropes and rollers completely out of the question.

Barcode of the Beast

In that quadrant of cyberspace where extreme right politics meet religious fundamentalism, courtesy of state-of-the-art computer technology, the belief has grown that the federal government will shortly force us to be tattooed with a barcode of a soft injectable plastic, either on our foreheads or on the backs of our right hands. The code will contain all the relevant data of our lives, from our credit status to our criminal records. The belief not only provides reinforcement to the perception that the feds—and their sinister shadow masters in **The New World Order**—are a demonic force in the land, but it also fulfills one of the End Time prophesies in the **Book of Revelation**. "He also forced all, the small and the great, and the rich and the poor, and the free and the slaves, to receive a mark upon their right hand or upon their forehead; so that none would be able to buy or sell, except those possessing the mark"—Revelation 13:15-17

Bavarian Illuminati

Although the secret society known as the Bavarian Illuminati has been around since the eighteenth century, it really made its mark on twentieth-century pop culture in the 1970s with the "Illuminatus" series of highly paranoid science fiction/fantasy novels by Robert Shea and Robert Anton Wilson. Because these books were essentially based in historical fact, then extended outward into all manner of conspiratorial fantasy, they not only immediately gained a cult popularity, but at the same time, the Illuminati became instant players in many of the great global conspiracy theories. Some, like the notorious Commander X, author of *The Cosmic Patriot Files*, who circulate in the UFO and conspiracy underground, put forward the proposition that the Illuminati controlled the **CIA**, the KGB, the world banking system, **The New World Order** and were the ultimate hidden power behind just about everything that went on. Their influence penetrated to the fact that the "eye-in-the-pyramid" symbol used by the Illuminati appears on the one-dollar bill, indicating to some that the Illuminati have fully infiltrated not only the Federal Reserve but perhaps the entire federal government.

The Bavarian Illuminati were founded on May 1, 1776, by Adam Weishaupt, a young professor at the University of Ingoldstat. Weishaupt had studied the ancient pagan religions as an undergraduate. After a later and seemingly disappointing flirtation with **Freemasonry**, he resolved to create the ultimate secret society that would represent Weishaupt's almost proto-communist political dream of a utopian superstate in which private property, social authority, nationality, and organized religion would all be abolished. There, in a condition of sublime anarchy, human beings would live in a harmonious universal brotherhood based on free love, peace, spiritual wisdom, and absolute equality.

Originally known as the Order of Perfectibilists, the Illuminati got off to a slow start but then started to gather momentum with lodges forming all across Germany and France, and more importantly, with Illuminati agents managing to infiltrate the power structure of Western Europe. One agent was reputedly the Comte de Mirabeau, a credited architect of the French Revolution. After the fall and execution of King Louis XVI, the Illuminati formed ties with the Society of Jacobins, one of the most radical and bloodthirsty of the revolutionary factions, and decided the next best move would be to foment revolution and bring down the monarchies all across Western Europe. With this aim in mind, the Illuminati began depositing large sums of money in banks in Amsterdam, London, Milan, and Paris to underwrite future uprisings. Acting as agents for the Illuminati were the great international banking family the House of Rothschild, who were already under suspicion of having financed the French Revolution.

The Illuminati appear to have infiltrated the United States even before there was one, forming Masonic-style lodges in each of the thirteen colonies. Through the nineteenth century, they are reputed to have quietly spread their tentacles across Europe using various Masonic orders as fronts. They formed links with the Serbian Order of the Black Hand, which was behind the murder of Archduke Franz Ferdinand and his wife, Sophia, in Sarajevo in 1914. The shooting of the royal couple by Gavrilo Princip, a tubercular student with only months to live, provided the flashpoint for World War I, which was in line with the avowed intent of the Illuminati to destroy all monarchies. As a result of the war, the royal houses of Germany, Russia, Turkey, Austria, and a number of smaller Balkan countries were replaced with either republics or dictatorships.

In the aftermath of the conflict, it's claimed that the Illuminati were also instrumental in influencing Adolf Hitler and the embryonic Nazi Party, although they might have to fight over that dubious credit with **Ordo Templi Orientis**. They also seemed to have consolidated their power in the U.S. through the duration of the Roosevelt New Deal to the point where, in 1935, FDR and his Secretary of Agriculture, Henry Wallace, were able to pull off the so-called conspiracy to put the Illuminati eye-in-the-pyramid logo on the U.S. one-dollar bill. America and its currency were thus forever branded as Illuminati turf. Roosevelt himself has been accused of being a member of the Ancient Arab Order of Nobles and Mystics, an Illuminati offshoot that counted among its members Mirabeau, Frederick the Great of Prussia, Goethe, Spinoza, Kant, Sir Francis Bacon, and Garibaldi. During the era of the Red witchhunts, it was claimed that Roosevelt's mission for the organization was to introduce into American life the social and political tenants of what was known as "crypto-communism"—the form of communism that conquered by stealth and deception.

Conspiracists claim that since World War II, after acting as midwife at the birth of the CIA, the Illuminati continue their nefarious and mysterious work through front organizations like the Tri-lateral Commission, the **Council for Foreign Relations** and the **Bilderburg Group**. They are even linked with **Majestic 12** and the sellout of the Earth to the grey aliens. As if that wasn't enough, the Bavarian Illuminati are also tagged as the force behind the **JFK assassination**, not because they had any particular beef with Jack Kennedy, but because his murder constituted an occult sacrifice of "The

Divine King." Although according to one school of mysticism, Kennedy ought to have been allowed to hold power for the statutory seven years. The Illuminati also figure in some of the more peripheral Marilyn Monroe scenarios, again as the ritual sacrifice of the temporal fertility goddess. Fortunately, no one has yet claimed that it was the Illuminati who got **Elvis**, although now that the idea is planted, we may only have to wait until it comes back to us as stated reality.

BEAST

According to Californian psychic and conspiracy theorist Sean David Morton—who also claims to have identified the **Antichrist**—**Area 51** in Nevada is not only the home to secret experimental aircraft, UFOs, and live aliens but also a Quantum super computer—Battle Engagement Area Simulation and Tracking. BEAST is the next generation of Global Positioning Systems, mind-control weaponry, and the ability to tag and track every human being on Earth with Multi-Automated Reader Chips (MARC). Thus, the biblical "Mark of the Beast" in **The Book of Revelation**, becomes the technological MARC of the BEAST.

Beatles, The

"The Beatles have been a real force for anti-American spirit." Thus spake **Elvis Presley** at his historic 1970 Oval Office meeting with President Richard Nixon. Before he and Nixon posed for pictures, Elvis went on to explain how The Beatles had waged a heinous campaign to subvert the teens of the U.S. by turning them on to **marijuana** and then to harder drugs. At least Elvis had the excuse that he was stoned out of his mind and trying to impress Nixon sufficiently so that the president would make him an honorary DEA agent and give him a badge for his collection.

The reason for the resurgence of this idea of The Beatles as agents of subversion in the 1990s is a little harder to explain. Currently, it's being promoted by Webster Tarpley, who heads a Washington consultancy operation called the Schuler Institute, the services of which are apparently used by a number of senators and congresspersons. It's only when deeper digging reveals the Schuler Institute is connected to that old political rogue, Lyndon Larouche—who, among his other extreme beliefs, maintains that the Queen of England, Elizabeth II, secretly controls the international traffic in narcotics—that it all begins to make a kind of distorted sense.

Bennewitz, Paul

The bizarre story of Paul Bennewitz has become a celebrated horror tale among the hard core of UFO conspiracy buffs. Dr. Paul Bennewitz was a physicist and inventor with a passion for UFO research. Using the best high-tech equipment at his disposal, he filmed and recorded the repeated appearances of odd, erratically moving lights in the sky over Kirkland Air Force Base in New Mexico during the late 1970s. Calling his work Project Beta, Bennewitz amassed over 2600 feet of film and many hours of audio transmissions that he firmly believed were messages from the strange flying lights.

In 1979, he was contacted by psychologist Dr. Leo Sprinkle to assist in the case of a badly disturbed female patient who, via hypnotic regression treatment, was apparently revealed to have been **abducted by aliens**. After a considerable period of study, Bennewitz and Sprinkle came to the conclusion that the patient had been more than just the victim of an abduction by aliens. An electronic mind-control device was implanted in her skull, enabling the aliens to see what she saw and hear what she heard.

At this point, however, the Paul Bennewitz story seemed to go totally off the rails. He rapidly evolved the theory—based on his Project Beta work and the consultations with Sprinkle—that two opposing forces of aliens had invaded the Earth. On one side, "white aliens" were benign, peaceful, and had come to this planet to extend the hand of intergalactic brotherhood. On the other side, "grey aliens," malevolent and sinister, were responsible for all the alien related nastiness—the abductions, the **cattle mutilation**, the electronic implants—happening in the world. The greys had formed an alliance with groups within the U.S. government, and in return for advanced technology, these officials allowed them to set up an underground base beneath Archuleta Peak near Dulce, New Mexico. After decoding what he believed were alien radio transmissions, Bennewitz became convinced that the greys and their human collaborators had fallen into conflict, the secret treaty was about to be broken, and total interplanetary war was imminent. Bennewitz believed that it was his mission to warn the world. As well as telling his story to other UFO theorists, he attempted to contact senators, congressmen, the Pentagon, and even the president.

It might have been possible to dismiss Bennewitz as just another nut with a paranoid delusion that the sky was falling. Unfortunately, we also have the testimony of William Moore that makes it, if not harder, certainly more complicated to dismiss Bennewitz out of hand. William Moore has, for almost twenty years, been a player in the shadow world of extraterrestrial paranoia. Moore is the author of a book on the supposed flying saucer crash near **Roswell**, New Mexico, and one of the team who supposedly received the ultra-secret **Majestic 12** papers that, if genuine, revealed government/alien complicity. Another of Moore's claims to fame is that he was recruited to work with a group of agents from a number of Federal agencies—coordinated by the Air Force Office of Special Investigations (AFOSI). They were feeding Paul Bennewitz what purported to be more official secret documents and audiotapes related to the alien invasion. This information was designed to fuel his paranoia and had the ultimate goal of driving him completely over the edge of sanity, a goal that was achieved when an exhausted Bennewitz was finally hospitalized.

To the dispassionate observer, it might seem that Bennewitz was crazy enough already without government efforts to make him worse. Moore claims he was never told why Bennewitz had become the target of such a malicious disinformation campaign, but he presents two possible options. The first is that Bennewitz was a harmless, but unlucky nut who had been chosen, almost at random, as the subject of an inter-agency training exercise in psychological warfare operation (psyops). The second is that while filming the lights over the Kirkland base, Bennewitz had stumbled across something that, while not a secret collaboration with dangerous aliens, was still something the government didn't want made public.

Berosus

In the second century B.C., Berosus, the Chaldean astronomer, prophesied that a disastrous planetary alignment in July of the year 2000 would cause nearly all life on Earth to be destroyed in a catastrophic fire. The surviving few would perish in an equally all-consuming flood in October of that year when the same planets are realigned in Capricorn—a severe case of "if the right one don't get you, the left one will," and one of the earliest predictions that it all stops with the end of the second Christian millennium.

Bible on the Moon

In early 1995, Terrence Cunningham, a Palo Alto, California, Unitarian minister, embarked on what he estimated was a $70 million fund-raising campaign to build a rocketship and lunar-landing vehicle for the purpose of placing an indestructible copy of the Holy Bible on the moon for safekeeping. Cunningham told the newspaper *Mountain View Voice* that the Bible would be preserved against tampering or, in case civilization is destroyed on Earth from plagues, wars, or in his words, "acts of God." Since that time, no follow-up reports have been forthcoming.

Bilderburg Group

Along with the Tri-lateral Commission and the **Council for Foreign Relations**, the Bilderburg Group is looked upon by many on the right, including the more theoretical arms of the militia movement, as one of the major manipulators of world affairs, the dedicated enemy of U.S. national sovereignty, and perhaps a clandestine prototype for the dreaded World

Government. Founded in May 1954, allegedly with financing from the **CIA**, the group's first meeting took place at the Bilderburg Hotel in Osterbeck, Holland, from which it took its name. Its first chairman was Prince Bernhard of the Netherlands, who retained the position until 1974, when his involvement in the Lockheed Aircraft Corporation scandal forced him to resign in favor of ex-British Prime Minister, Sir Alec Douglas-Home. The group has no official membership list, but at least once a year, it meets behind closed doors. Eighty to one hundred of the West's richest and most influential power brokers, including politicians, financiers, and media barons attend. Most are reputed to be of a conservative ideological bent and strongly anti-communist. This fact, however, doesn't seem to sway the grassroots rightists who see the group as purely malevolent.

The fact that the details of what takes place at these meetings are strictly secret also provides considerable leeway for all manner of conspiracy theories. Some Bilderburg watchers make much of the fact that, in 1976, fifteen representatives of the Soviet Union attended a Bilderburg meeting in the Arizona desert at a time that exactly coincided with President Jimmy Carter's new policy of *détente*. Was World Government extending itself eastward?

At the furthest extreme, the truly paranoid see the Bilderburg Group as nothing more than a front for the **Bavarian Illuminati**, with definite occult undertones. They cite the fact that 39 individuals comprise the Bilderburg steering committee and 39 equals 13 + 13 + 13, and as we all know, the number thirteen has a number of mystic associations. Tenuous maybe, but conspiracy scenarios can be constructed from any smidgen of fact when need be.

Black Avenger, The

Since the late 1980s, the Black Avenger has been a legendary and highly sinister figure in the world of computer hackers. The uncorroborated but often repeated story is that the Albanian-based super-hacker, working on primitive, black market technology from the former Soviet space program, has issued a number of communiqués claiming—among other acts of cyber-sabotage—that he destroyed an Ethiopian water production plant by scrambling its computer programs. His last communiqué, sent in 1995, threatened that he would attempt to take down the air traffic control system of a major airport, causing a multiple plane disaster and massive loss of life.

Black Cocaine

A new ruse by the Colombian drug cartels to thwart law enforcement is to mix cocaine with cobalt and ferric chloride. The resulting black powder, known as *coca negra*, has no distinctive odor and cannot be rooted out by sniffer dogs. Before being made available to customers, the cobalt and ferric chloride can be washed out with solvents, restoring the drug to its original pristine whiteness. Colombian police chief Roso Jose Serrano takes almost a wry pride in this piece of national ingenuity. "For good or bad, Colombians have a boundless ingenuity."

Black Helicopters

Black Helicopters could almost be classified as a third generation of mutant paranoia. In the beginning, or at least in the early 1960s, we had the Men in Black, later abbreviated to MIBs. The MIBs were the not quite human version of the Blues Brothers who showed up to instill silence-inducing fear into UFO witnesses or contactees. When stories of the MIBs first started to circulate, opinion was divided as to whether they were actual aliens doing their own dirty spin control or whether they were agents of some shadowy government agency in cahoots with the ETs. One factor about which there was no disagreement was that the MIBs drove mysterious black Cadillacs, models that were at least ten years old but smelled and looked brand-spanking showroom new.

From the standpoint of cultural anthropology, the Black Helicopters seem to be a direct descendant of the MIB's Cadillac, and like the MIBs themselves, they have become the subject of some controversy as different groups attempt to claim them as their own. Initially, they were the preserve of the **cattle mutilation** people, who claimed that shortly before laser-mutilated cattle were discovered in remote rural areas, silent black helicopters were observed hightailing it out of Montana or South Dakota. The neo-fascist fringe then adopted the Black Helicopters. They still had their muffled, almost silent engines but were now of an anti-radar, stealth-style design and appeared to be the favorite weapons of United Nations Special Forces. Fronting for **The New World Order**, they were setting up bases all over the United States—using troops on loan from Pakistan and Turkey—getting ready for the suspension of the Constitution and the great overthrow of America.

The UFO people couldn't very well take this lying down. The Black Helicopters were theirs. Hadn't they been seen flying escort to the reverse- engineered flying saucers buzzing around **Area 51** in the Nevada high desert? Even the UFO believers, however, couldn't quite agree on some of the details. Were the Black Helicopters of human origin, the state of the art in dirty tricks aviation, or were they alien constructs, essentially UFOs in disguise? The obvious compromise, offered by those who were prepared to accept the existence of such machines but who did not want to join any special-interest group, was that Black Helicopters were a Pentagon black projects construct, perhaps part of the stealth program—now standard transportation for any number of different ultra-covert operations.

The band Soul Coughing has validated the Black Helicopter fascination by recording a song, "Black Helicopters," that was included on the CD *Songs in the Key of X,* a spin-off compilation album that is part of the merchandizing of the TV show **The X-Files**.

Black Knight Satellite

The early days of the US/Soviet space race in the late 1950s saw Russia and America both attempt to launch relatively small satellites weighing little more than a few hundred pounds. Thus, on January 4, 1960, when astronomers and tracking stations detected two very large connected objects, perhaps with a gross collective weight of nearly thirty tons, describing a perfect polar orbit around the Earth, their alarm and consternation was more than understandable. After a month of tracking the objects amid gathering rumor and speculation, the U.S. Department of Defense formally announced that an unidentified satellite was circling the Earth. Confirmation also came directly from Moscow. Dr. Alla Masevitch, the Soviet scientist who headed up the Sputnik tracking program, denied the mysterious satellite was one of theirs.

The story was carried by, among others, the *New York Times*, *Newsweek*, and *Life*, and the media christened the object "The Black Knight." After doing nothing but silently maintaining its orbit for a number of months, the Black Knight vanished just as mysteriously as it had arrived. It wasn't gone for good though. The Black Knight continues to show up periodically, although these days, its visits are never publicized. They are recorded, however, in the fine print of NASA's weekly catalog of all the objects floating in nearby space and can be found by anyone who cares to look.

Black Vulcans

Black Vulcans—a name derived from the British Avro Vulcan delta-winged atom bombers of the 1950s—has become the popular tag given to vast triangular UFOs with a bright light at each of their three corners. Over the past eight years they have been regularly appearing in skies over the British Isles and Northern Europe. In 1989, two Belgium Air Force F-16 fighters locked on to a "Black Vulcan" that then proceeded to behave in a manner impossible for any conventional aircraft, even the U.S. experimental class of stealth planes. Unlike most of the world's military, Belgian authorities were perfectly open about the highly alien nature of these craft, and Belgian Defense Minister Guy Coeme actually released the tapes from the F-16's black box flight records, demonstrating that the craft could hardly have been of any known terrestrial origin.

Bob Dylan's Motorcycle

A classic conspiracy theory of the hippie era was that when Bob Dylan was involved in a motorcycle accident near his home in Woodstock in 1966, and subsequently made no public performances for almost four years, the **CIA** had rigged the bike to crash in order to neutralize Dylan's influence on the youth of America. Later biographers have suggested that the accident was, in fact, not particularly serious, but Dylan had used it as an excuse to withdraw from the spotlight and recover from a major drug habit.

Book of Lies, The

Published in 1912 by British occult leader Aleister Crowley, apparently in complete contravention of the rules of the **Ordo Templi Orientis** that he headed at the time, *The Book of Lies* was a coded instruction manual in various methods, rites, and practices of sexual magic. These included one technique whereby prolonged and mutual oral sex could be used as a form of occult meditation. By all accounts, *The Book of Lies* was chock full o' fun, but the kicker was that you first had to crack the highly complex and symbolic code.

Book of Revelation, The

In its time, the Book of Revelation has inspired a great deal of Christian mysticism and poetry and caused a good deal of trouble. It has been a favorite source of biblical inspiration for a range of the dangerously devoted and seekers of holy horror, from the Salem witchhunters through countless hellfire evangelists to David Koresh and Charles Manson. In a coldly rational perspective, The Book of Revelation is the short, science fiction finale of the New Testament. It was apparently written during the latter part of the first century, during the reign of the Roman Emperor Domitian (81–96 A.D.). The writer simply calls himself John, but the common and traditional acceptance is that this is the Apostle John, at the time imprisoned in a Roman penal colony for political offenders on the Greek island of Patmos in the southeast Aegean. Even accepting that the birth of Jesus Christ took place at the start of the Christian calendar, and that he was crucified in Jerusalem in 33 A.D., certain problems arise concerning the authorship. If the writer of Revelation was one of the original twelve disciples, he would have been an exceptionally old man when he wrote down his vision, well past the average lifespan of the first century, and miraculously past the life expectancy of any Roman political prisoner.

The plotline of Revelation is all but incoherent, concerned with the events that come into play when each of a set of mystic seals are opened. The Seven Seals are broken. The first four Seals let loose the well-known and very familiar Four Horsemen of the Apocalypse—Death, War, Famine, and Pestilence. The fifth Seal brings a Great Tribulation. The breaking of the sixth Seal heralds weird happenings in the skies. With the breaking of the seventh Seal, all hell quite literally breaks loose. At this point, seven equally mystic trumpets sound, the Great Beast takes over the Earth, humanity suffers seven devastating plagues, followed by earthquakes, fires, and hail, the seas and rivers are choked with pollution and run with blood. Two hundred million horsemen engage in battle, and one-third of humanity is killed. With the sounding of the final, seventh trumpet, Jesus Christ comes again, bringing the flying city of the New Jerusalem, and the faithful are saved. As one noted theologian put it, "Revelation is the great wish fulfillment. Everything is resolved in one final and terrible act of violence. Satan is vanquished and thrown into the lake of burning sulfur. Sinners are utterly destroyed."

Even the early Christians had some doubts about the violence of Revelation, and it was almost expunged from the original Hebrew and Greek texts. It only truly came into its own when the Emperor Constantine adopted Christianity as the official religion of the Roman war machine in 312 A.D. It also figured prominently when, in the early fifth century, St. Augustine developed the philosophical concept of the "just war." In all respects, Revelation completely negates the original Christian message of peace, love, and harmony between men and concentrates on the hideous threatening of those who refuse to embrace the author's belief systems. It returns to the Old Testament concept of a foul-tempered and surprisingly fallible God who, seeing how badly he has failed in his endeavors to create a universe inhabited by a species fashioned in his own image, petulantly destroys all that he has made. John essentially postulated a God so dangerously psychotic that almost anything could be perpetrated in his name.

John's claim in Revelation 1:10 is that he was actually transported to the future where he observed, from a safe vantage point, the final battle between good and evil and the ultimate judgement of mankind by God. A popular 1960s take on Revelation was that John was experiencing a form of psychedelic vision induced by the ingestion of hallucinogenic mushrooms. The cynic's viewpoint is that John was simply driven crazy by incarceration in a Roman gulag. The more mystic UFO buffs have suggested that John was taken by flying saucer to have his mind blown on some other planet, or that time-traveling aliens simply let him have a good look at something like the battlefields of World War I, which were simply more than his first-century consciousness could relate to.

Branch Davidians

For almost a hundred years, the Branch Davidians were a small and obscure apocalyptic sect. Then they were taken over by David Koresh and turned into Jim Jones's **People's Temple** to die at the hands of the FBI in full paramilitary force. They were essentially a disgruntled spin-off of the Seventh Day Adventists, prone to sex scandals and hierarchical infighting, who kept predicting the end of the world and then falling into confusion when the end failed to materialize. If they hadn't been incinerated by the federal government's tanks and helicopters at the end of the fifty-one-day siege in 1993 at their Mount Carmel commune outside of Waco, Texas, they might never have become the holy martyrs of the extreme right they are today.

Bubonic Plague

Larry Harris, a septic-tank operator from Dubin, Ohio, and a member of the extreme neo-Nazi organization the Aryan Nation, was charged in 1995 with purchasing vials of freeze-dried bubonic plague under false pretenses. He had obtained the plague vials from American Type Culture Collection, a supply company specializing in servicing private-sector bacteriological research. He had told them that he owned a lab and was a serious researcher. Seemingly, his word had been taken without question.

C

Carter, Jimmy

Jimmy Carter is the only president of the United States, living or dead, who openly admits to having experienced a UFO sighting.

Castro, Fidel

One of the great paranoias in the conspiracy world of shadows is that the **Central Intelligence Agency** is omnipotent, unbeatable, and running everything. The logical antidote to that kind of mental helplessness is to remember Cuban leader Fidel Castro. Although the CIA has, since 1960, made the overthrow of the Castro regime one of its highest priorities, Fidel still remains in power. For three years, under the code name Operation Mongoose, the agency tried to kill him with such exotic devices as exploding and poisoned cigars, other kinds of toxins, a sabotaged scuba suit, and an exploding exotic seashell (Castro was a skin diving enthusiast). All attempts failed, as did the non-lethal efforts to destabilize the revolutionary government that were substituted after John Kennedy, shortly before his own assassination, banned the attempts to kill Castro.

Cattle Mutilation

One of the big-ticket weird horrors of the 1970s and 1980s was the furor over cattle mutilation, but it appears to have died down during the 1990s without any real resolution. The bizarre phenomenon of dead cattle left on the open range in many of the prairie states was blamed on a number of causes. UFO researchers claimed it was the result of alien genetic research. Writer Ed Sanders and movie director Alan Rudolph, in his 1982 film *Endangered Species*, both figured it was the work of renegade bio-warfare researchers carrying on "black" experiments when their work had been officially outlawed by the government. Christian groups, on the other hand, saw it as the work of Satanic cultists.

Unless the mutilations start up again in large numbers, we may never know. A fascinating little postscript recently surfaced, however, when Dr. Henry Monteith, a retired Scandia Laboratories engineering physicist, discovered that Native Americans had determinedly avoided the carcasses of mutilated cattle and immediately buried them when they were discovered on Indian land. "They don't say anything about it because it's being done by the 'sky people'."

CBS

CBS television changed its corporate logo to a large graphic eye at about the same time George Bush made his post-Gulf War "victory" speech announcing the arrival of a **New World Order**. Many right-wing conspiracists referred to the fact that the CBS symbol could be seen as an adaptation of the **Bavarian Illuminati**/Masonic eye-in-the-pyramid, and that George Bush is reputed to be a thirty-third degree Mason and a member of the Yale Skull and Bones Club. They took it to be a covert announcement of a total **Illuminati**/Masonic takeover of the U.S.

Cell Phones

Are cell phones prone to cause brain tumors? The most recent research by an Australian team, headed by Dr. Michael Repacholi at the Royal Adelaide Hospital, seems to indicate that this may be the case. In experiments that exposed a number of genetically-engineered, cancer-susceptible mice to the kind of electro**magnetic** fields that become established around a mobile phone user's head, 43 percent of the mice developed cancer rather than the expected 22 percent.

By way of a related cultural sidebar, could the cell phone that she uses so much be the real reason Agent Dana Scully developed a brain tumor on the 1996–97 series of The **X-Files**?

Central Intelligence Agency

Through all the labyrinths of conspiracy and paranoia that have expanded their twists, turns, blind alleys, and complexities through the second half of the twentieth century, it is almost impossible to make a move without either stumbling over the Central Intelligence Agency or at least finding traces of what appears to be its handiwork. Other government agencies have, at times, suffered a bad rap. The Internal Revenue Service has been regularly castigated for a supposed lack of humanity. The FBI under **J. Edgar Hoover** was accused of becoming the American Secret Police. In the aftermath of the **Branch Davidian** siege at Waco, the Bureau of Alcohol, Tobacco, and Firearms found itself the number one enemy of the right-wing militia movement. The CIA, however, almost since it was established in 1947 as a permanent replacement for the World War II Office of Strategic Services (OSS), has been demonized and held responsible for maybe half the evils on this planet.

It certainly cannot be denied that the agency, known by both friends and foes alike as "The Company," has largely itself to blame for its unpopularity. Its obsession with secrecy and the cowboy arrogance with which it conducted many of its covert—and even not so covert—operations made it vulnerable to massive public distrust and paranoid speculation. If we assume for a moment that the CIA had nothing to do with the **assassination of John F. Kennedy**, the simple fact that so many rational, honest, tax-paying Americans firmly believe that it did can only indicate the quantum credibility gap the agency has created for itself.

It would be a mistake, though, to assume the CIA is a coherent and monolithic organization, always acting with one accord and a single objective. In many respects, the agency has been the victim of the sum of its parts, and the product of what were, at the time, temporary and pragmatic expediencies that became ingrained and institutionalized. In the aftermath of World War II, it seemed to be a good idea—via what became known as Operation Paperclip—to recruit Nazi intelligence agents from the Gestapo and the SS, such as the notorious **Gehlen** group, for their knowledge of Soviet spy systems in the newly occupied Iron Curtain countries. Unfortunately, that kind of deal with the Devil is very much a two-way street, and certain elements of the Nazi mindset began to be incorporated in the worst Company attitudes.

In the same way, the doctrinaire anti-communism of Director Allen Dulles, who ran the agency through the Eisenhower administration—until he was fired by President Kennedy after the failure of the aborted Bay of Pigs invasion of Cuba—set patterns of CIA behavior that have long outlived their usefulness. They have, over the years, repeatedly embarrassed Americans. From the almost forty years of the undeclared CIA war on **Fidel Castro**'s Cuba to the continuing accusations that the agency is still heavily involved in the global narcotics business, the agency refuses to shake itself loose from an outmoded, Cold War world view. The Dulles doctrine, which would later be resurrected by Oliver North during the **Reagan** years, that enemies of one's enemies must, by definition, be one's friends has caused the CIA to form some less than comfortable alliances. The support of too many extreme right military dictatorships, the overthrow of democratically elected, moderate socialist governments, as happened in Guatemala, Iran, and Chile, and the kind of torture and murder sanctioned by **Operation Phoenix** in Vietnam and taught at the **School of the Americas** at Fort Benning, Georgia, have all but divorced the CIA—in the opinion of much of the world—from the very basic U.S. principles of freedom and democracy. This seeming contradiction has caused many observers to suspect that the Company was, and perhaps still is, following its own independent political agenda and making its own foreign policy.

The latest piece of pragmatism that seems to be returning to haunt the agency is the CIA's former support of the Mujaheddin Moslem fundamentalist guerrillas in Afghanistan. When the Mujaheddin were fighting the Red Army during the Soviet occupation of their country, they received all the assistance in terms of weapons, finance, and advisors that they could handle. The Stinger anti-aircraft missiles supplied to them by the CIA almost totally neutralized the Russians' offensive use of helicopter gunships and turned the tide of the conflict. Today, with the Soviets long gone and the U.S.—the "Great Satan"—now the primary foe, the self-same weapons supplied by the CIA back in the 1980s may not be directly turned on cities and citizens in the U.S. But they will definitely be employed to protect the opium crops that the Mujaheddin are now cultivating with the avowed intent of flooding Europe and America with cheap potent heroin—an adjunct to bringing down the decadent culture of the "western infidels."

Although no one rationally expects a national intelligence agency to function with complete openness, the CIA maintains a cult of secrecy that it wraps around itself like a cloak of invisibility. Secrecy is maintained to such a degree that Representative Norman Mineta of the House Intelligence Committee once bitterly remarked, "we are like mushrooms, they keep us in the dark and feed us a lot of manure." All too often, the Company seems to be using secrecy less to confuse potential enemies than to hide its activities from possible congressional and public oversight. Many of the bizarre experimental drug and mind- control programs like **MKULTRA** were conducted without any kind of governmental knowledge and were only publicly and partially revealed after lengthy and probing investigations such as the

1975 Rockefeller Commission. Another area where the CIA has generated a wealth of citizen paranoia is with regard to its operations inside the United States.

When the CIA was founded, many national leaders, including FBI Director J. Edgar Hoover, feared that the agency could all too easily, if not brought under considerable control, be turned into a "U.S. Gestapo." One of the agreed checks and balances was that the CIA was not permitted to either spy on the American people or conduct domestic intelligence operations (that was left to the FBI). For practical purposes, a few grey areas were allowed to remain in the agency's charter. Obviously, the CIA wasn't going to halt surveillance on a suspect simply because he or she had entered U.S. territory. All through the 1950s, these grey areas were progressively exploited, ignored, and consciously overstepped. By the Vietnam era, the CIA's Operation CHAOS was routinely and illegally spying on large numbers of U.S. citizens, attempting to prove a link between the anti-war movement and either the Soviet government or that of Red China.

Despite the attempts in the wake of Watergate to reform the CIA, the dossiers that it maintains on U.S. citizens are still one of its most closely guarded secrets. In 1975, John Tunney, chairman of the Subcommittee on Constitutional Rights, charged that the agency had detailed dossiers on over 100,000 Americans—including a list of some 15,000 who would be immediately arrested in the event of a national emergency. These were stored at the massive underground computer complex at **Mount Weather** near Bluemont, Virginia. Those dossiers have neither been removed nor destroyed, and there is every reason to believe that since that time they have only been added to.

As we enter the twenty-first century, many, like Senator Daniel Patrick Moynihan, are seriously asking—when we have spy satellites that can supposedly photograph a car license plate from orbit—do we need a Central Intelligence Agency at all, especially one still constituted and organized according to the needs of the Cold War? On the other hand, the CIA, with its network of alliances and secret treaties, its connections in world narcotics, and its own private banks and airlines might not be so easy to dismantle.

Charlie Manson's Web Site

Charlie Manson was always the technical innovator. In the late 1960s, just prior to his arrest for the Tate/La Bianca murders, he was allegedly perfecting the dune buggy attack vehicle at his hideout in Death Valley. In tune with the cybernetic mode of the 1990s, Charlie now has a Web site. When the media got wind of this in the early part of 1997, they immediately became sensationally bent out of shape at the prospect that cyber-Satanism and the Evil of Manson should be propagated among young people on the Internet—a medium still misunderstood and subconsciously feared by a lot of the tabloids. As they told it, we might wake up one bright morning and find that Helter Skelter II had come to pass and that the United States was taken over by computer-generated psychedelic, killer zombies. All in all, the response to the Manson Web site was akin—only more so—to the teacup storm that blew up in the late 1980s when a company called Mother Productions started manufacturing and selling serial killer trading cards.

What the tabloid media didn't grasp, or more likely, neglected to tell us, was that Charlie doesn't actually run his own Web pages. No one in a California maximum-security prison is allowed to do that. The site is run by Manson enthusiasts and is fairly tame compared to many of the weirder sites out on the Internet edge. Another major omission was that a Manson Family Web site was virtually inevitable. Charlie has been a cottage industry ever since his 1970–71 trial, and since that time, dozens of books, underground comics, audio and videocassettes, T-shirts, and all manner of paraphernalia have been in circulation. Manson Web pages were nothing more than a logical continuation of ongoing Manson marketing.

Something else the media managed to ignore is that far from just one Manson site, dozens of them now exist on the Web. They carry all manner of Manson Family trivia, like the *TV and Radio Urban Legends* site that includes an item about how there is no truth in a long-running rumor, apparently first generated by KROQ DJ Rodney Biggenheimer, that Manson auditioned for the Monkees.

Perhaps the biggest absurdity is that the tabloid media are regularly outraged that there should be Manson enthusiasts, multiple Manson Web sites, or a Manson industry at all—and yet, they've played a considerable part in the creation of all three. They have always been aware of the power of the Manson name to draw ratings, and in the heyday of shows like *A Current Affair* and *Hard Copy*, no sweeps period went by without at least one segment on the Family. The tabloid hysteria that Charlie was either the devil incarnate or the dark side of flower power was maintained through all the anniversaries and reevaluations of the murders—all the interviews with Charlie by Geraldo Rivera, Tom Snyder, Charlie Rose, et al. That publicity, plus the mandatory airtime each time Charlie or one of his women came up for a parole hearing, did a great deal to keep him in the public eye and make him the celebrity mass killer he remains today.

Chernobyl Containment Structure

The Chernobyl sarcophagus, the vast concrete and steel structure built just five years ago with the labor of over 600,000 people and designed to last for centuries—if not millennia—is already starting to collapse. Walls are buckling and holes and large cracks have appeared. A new, much larger tomb for the destroyed former-Soviet nuclear power station may have to be built over it. The prognosis for being able to successfully seal the disaster site without further release of radiation is not good. The original reactor building still contains large quantities of "hot" radioactive material and, just to complicate matters, the internal robot monitoring systems have failed and are permanently down. Human volunteers—known as "jumpers" in the nuke business—now have to conduct all internal inspections, absorbing massive doses of radiation in the process. Many are already showing symptoms of cancer and acute radiation sickness.

Chupacabra

The word "chupacabra" is Spanish for goat sucker. While the U.S. and Northern Europe find themselves plagued by alien abductors and high-tech UFOs, the Latin world falls victim to the less grandiose depredations of this large-eyed, long-clawed, snaggle-toothed, roughly-humanoid, bipedal, and seemingly vampiric being. It attacks domestic animals like goats, sheep and cattle, some small children, and the occasional adult, sucking the blood and internal organs from its victims. Chupacabras have shown up primarily in Mexico, where they have caused a number of mass panics in rural areas, and in Honduras, Puerto Rico, Spain, Italy, and North Africa. The two main and opposing explanations so far are that the beings are either the result of some genetic engineering experiment gone hideously wrong, or else they are some bizarre extraterrestrial intruder. The latter explanation tends to question why an alien species, technically advanced enough to cross the massive distances between star systems, would arrive at an inhabited planet and immediately start sucking goats. Unless, of course, the chupacabra is a kind of subspecies, either an escaped alien pet or (by human standards) a particularly disgusting gatherer of organic samples. Whatever the answer, the chupacabra is assured of its place in UFO/scary monster mythology. It has already been the subject of an episode of **The X-Files**.

Church of Scientology, The

The Church of Scientology has many lawyers and they tend to sue anyone who says bad things about them.

Church Universal and Triumphant, The

With the horrors of Jonestown and Waco still relatively fresh in the collective memory, you might think the stock of charismatic preachers who attempt to marry religion and survivalism would be at an all-time low. Elizabeth Clare Prophet, leader of The Church Universal and Triumphant, however, seems to be doing fine, despite the fact that her followers have created a frighteningly David Koresh-like survival fortress in Montana's Paradise Valley, near Yellowstone National Park. Seemingly better funded and better organized than the Branch Davidians, their Royal Teton Ranch complex includes nuclear fallout shelters and enough stockpiled food to support several hundred of the faithful for up to seven years.

One of the major thrusts of Prophet's teachings is that we are already at the edge of the abyss. We have already entered "a period of intensification in all our lives and a disturbance in the elements" that will ultimately lead to the final—and in this case, nuclear—holocaust. When the dust has settled, the faithful will emerge from their bunkers and inherit the Earth. Although Prophet would probably be furious at the comparison, this aspect of her teaching leans perilously close to what Charlie Manson described in the post-Helter Skelter scenario to Squeaky, Linda, Sadie, and Tex.

Prophet does, however, use the Bible rather than **The Beatles**' White Album to support her position. "Moses told us to choose life, not death. I cannot choose to allow myself to die when I can save myself and my children." Neighboring Montana farmers (and let's not forget that this is also **cattle mutilation** country) have become understandably nervous when such statements go hand-in-hand with rumors that the Church Universal and Triumphant is also armed to the teeth.

Clinton Death List

Stories of how Bill Clinton came to power and stayed there over a growing pile of dead bodies have been circulating among the extreme right—and at times, the not so extreme right—at least since the election of 1996. The so-called "Clinton Death List" has circulated in rightist publications and militia movement newsletters for a number of years and has been mentioned in passing by Rush Limbaugh, G. Gordon Liddy, and other right-wing radio personalities. It finally started to surface at the end of 1998 as a circulating piece of chain e-mail. The following came from one of these pieces of e-mail, cyber-disinformation, and is reproduced as it appeared with the obvious disclaimer that there may not be a word of truth in it.

How would you like to be Bill Clinton's friend?

The following is a list of dead people connected with Bill Clinton.

James McDougal—Clinton's convicted Whitewater partner died of an apparent heart attack while in solitary confinement. He was a key witness in Ken Starr's investigation.

Mary Mahoney—Former White House intern who was murdered in July 1997 at a Starbuck's coffee shop in Georgetown just after she was to go public with her story of sexual harassment in the White House.

Vince Foster—Former White House councilor and colleague of Hillary Clinton at Little Rock's Rose law firm. Died of gunshot wound to the head, ruled a suicide.

Ron Brown—Secretary of Commerce and DNC Chairman. Reported to have died by impact in a plane crash. A pathologist close to the investigation of the accident reported that there was a hole in the top of Brown's skull resembling a gunshot wound. At the time of this death, Brown was being investigated for campaign fund violation and spoke publicly of his willingness to cut a deal with prosecutors.

C. Victor Raiser II and Montgomery Raiser—Major players in the Clinton fund-raising organization died in a private plane crash in July 1992.

Paul Tulley—Democratic National Committee political Director found dead in a hotel room in Little Rock, September 1992. Described by Clinton as a "dear friend and trusted advisor."

Ed Willey—Clinton fund raiser, found dead November 1993 deep in the woods in Virginia of a gunshot wound to the head. Ruled a suicide. Ed Willey died on the same day his wife Kathleen Willey claimed Bill Clinton groped her in the Oval Office of the White House. Ed Willey was involved in several Clinton fundraising events.

Jerry Parks—Head of Clinton's gubernatorial security team in Little Rock. Gunned down in his car at a deserted intersection outside Little Rock. Parks's son said his father was building a dossier on Clinton. He allegedly threatened to reveal this information. After he died, the files were mysteriously removed from his house.

James Bunch—Died from a gunshot suicide. It was reported that he had a "Black Book" of people who visited prostitutes in Texas and Arkansas.

James Wilson—Found dead in May 1993 from an apparent hanging suicide. He was reported to have ties to Whitewater.

Kathy Ferguson—Ex-wife of Arkansas State Trooper Danny Ferguson died in May, 1994. She was found dead in her living room with a gunshot wound to the head. It was ruled a suicide even though there were several packed suitcases as if she were going somewhere. Danny Ferguson was a codefendant along with Bill Clinton in the Paula Jones lawsuit. Kathy Ferguson was a possible corroborating witness for Paula Jones.

Bill Shelton—Arkansas State Trooper and fiancé of Kathy Ferguson. Critical of the suicide ruling on his fiancé, he was found dead of a gunshot wound, also ruled a suicide, at the gravesite of his fiancé.

Gandy Baugh—Attorney for Bill Clinton friend Dan Lassiter. He died by jumping out of a window of a tall building in January 1994. His client was a convicted drug distributor.

Florence Martin—Accountant subcontractor for the CIA. Related to the Barry Seals, Mena Airport drug smuggling case. Died of three gunshot wounds.

Suzanne Coleman—Reportedly had an affair with Clinton when he was Arkansas Attorney General. Died of a gunshot wound to the back of the head, ruled a suicide. Was pregnant at the time of her death.

Paula Grober—Clinton's speech interpreter for the deaf from 1978 until her death December 9, 1992. She died in a one-car accident.

Danny Casolaro—Investigative reporter. Investigating the cocaine smuggling through Mena Airport and the Arkansas Development Finance Authority. He slit his wrists, apparent suicide in the middle of his investigation.

Paul Wilcher—Attorney investigating corruption at Mena Airport and the 1980 "October Surprise" was found dead on a toilet June 22 in his Washington, D.C., apartment. He had delivered a report to Janet Reno three weeks before his death.

Jon Parnall Walker—Whitewater investigator for Resolution Trust Corp. who jumped to his death from his Arlington, Virginia, apartment balcony August 15, 1993. He was investigating Morgan Guarantee scandal.

Barbara Wise—Commerce Department staffer. Worked closely with Ron Brown and John Huang. Cause of death unknown. Died November 29, 1996. Her bruised nude body was found locked in her office at the Department of Commerce.

Charles Meissner—Assistant Secretary of Commerce, who gave John Huang special security clearance, died shortly thereafter in a small plane crash.

Dr. Stanley Heard—Chairman of the National Chiropractic Health Care Advisory Committee, died with attorney Steve Dickson in a small plane crash. Dr. Heard, in addition to serving on Clinton's advisory council personally treated Clinton's mother, stepfather, and brother.

Barry Seal—Drug-running pilot out of Mena Arkansas. Death was no accident.

Johnny Lawhorn, Jr.—Mechanic, found check made out to Clinton in the trunk of a car left in his repair shop. Died when his car hit a utility pole.

Stanley Huggins—Suicide. Investigated Madison Guarantee. His report was never released.

Hershell Friday—Attorney and Clinton fund raiser, died March 1, 1994 when his plane exploded.

Kevin Ives and Don Henry—known as, "The boys on the track case." Reports say the boys may have stumbled upon the Mena,

Arkansas airport drug operation. Controversial case where initial report said death was due to falling asleep on the railroad track. Later reports claim the two boys had been slain before being placed on the tracks. Many linked to the case died before their testimony could come before a grand Jury.

The following [seven] persons had information on the Ives/Henry case.

Keith Conay—Died when his motorcycle slammed into the back of a truck July 1988.

Keith McMaskle—Died when stabbed 113 times November 1989.

Gregory Collins—Died from gunshot wound January 1989.

Jeff Rhodes—He was shot, mutilated, and found burned to death in a trash dump in April 1989.

James Milan—Found decapitated. Coroner ruled death due to natural causes.

Jordan Kettleson—Found shot to death in the front seat of his pickup truck in June 1990.

Richard Winters—A suspect in the Ives/Henry deaths. Was killed in a setup robbery July 1989.

The following Clinton bodyguards are also dead: Major S. Barkley Jr., Captain Scott J. Reynolds, Sgt. Brian Hanley, Sgt. Tim Sabel, Major General William Robertson, Col. William Densburger, Col. Robert Kelly, Spec. Agents Gary Rose, Steve Willis, Robert Williams, Conway Le Bleu, and Todd McKeehan.

Cola

Yeah, we all know that there used to be cocaine in Coca-Cola, and late nineteenth-century hipsters would order a coke at a drug store with the words, "gimme a shot in the arm." But the Coca-Cola company took that out back in the 1900s because they figured it wasn't good for us. We also know that a human tooth left in a glass of coke for three or four days dissolves away to nothing, but that hardly counts because much the same thing happens to a tooth left in a glass of orange juice. What we only just discovered was that Coke, Pepsi, RC, Shasta, and the rest can also cause high blood pressure and heart attacks. Cola drinks contain high levels of phosphoric acid. Phosphoric acid bonds with magnesium, the body's natural protection against high blood pressure. When the phosphoric acid is excreted from the system, the magnesium goes right along with it and watch out heart!

Connally, John Bowden

A weird postscript/footnote to the **JFK assassination** was created when John Connally, the governor of Texas at the time of the murder, died on June 15, 1993. The Justice Department—prompted by a number of independent assassination researchers—attempted to obtain the fragments of the bullet that had lodged in Connally's wrist when he was riding directly in front of President Kennedy in the death car. The intention was to subject the bullet fragments to neutron-activation analysis and other tests to determine conclusively whether the fragments came from Warren Commission Exhibit 399—the so-called magic bullet that was supposed to have zigzagged through Kennedy's body and then exited to strike Connally in the wrist.

All through the rest of his life, Connally maintained that he definitely wasn't hit by the same bullet as the president, but by one that was fired seconds later—possibly from the roof of the Dallas County Records Building and not from the Texas Book Depository where Lee Harvey Oswald was allegedly shooting. **The Zapruder film** tends to confirm Connally's story, showing him still holding his Stetson hat in his supposedly injured hand well after Kennedy was hit.

The recovery of the bullet fragments could have thrown considerable light on one of the most controversial findings of the Warren Commission, but unfortunately it wasn't to be. The FBI was given the responsibility of handling the matter, but the agency made such a mess of it that anyone might be forgiven for suspecting its ineptitude was deliberate. FBI agents approached the Connally family *during* the governor's funeral, presumably wanting to open the coffin and extract the bullet right there and then. The horrified family naturally refused. The very next day, the FBI again contacted Connally's relatives for permission to now exhume the body and extract the fragments. Again the bereaved refused, this time angrily promising to "resist vigorously any efforts to disturb the body of John Connally." Thus, a vital key to the assassination was buried along with the ex-governor of Texas.

Council for Foreign Relations

Three names tend to appear over and over again in most of the conspiracy scenarios relating to World Government and **The New World Order**. These are the **Bilderburg Group**, the **Tri-lateral Commission** and the Council for Foreign Relations. Of the three, the CFR is distinguished as the oldest and possibly the most suspected, in some quarters, of widespread global chicanery. Originally formed in the aftermath of World War I and the Russian Revolution, the CFR was financed by wealthy international bankers and designed to act as a privately controlled shadow operation that would parallel the League of Nations. Its major concern was to counteract the spread of communism, and some critics accused it of covertly giving support and finance to Hitler and the emergent Nazi Party, although no proof of that has ever been produced. After World War II, the CFR, again according to its critics, did a 180-degree ideological turn and, through its support for the United Nations, began promoting international socialism and became the active arm of the New World Order. Some theorists even tie the CFR to **Majestic 12** and the supposed alien invaders currently working with the U.S. government. CFR members have supposedly included Adlai Stevenson, Hubert Humphrey, John Foster Dulles, Robert McNamara, Henry Kissinger, Nelson Rockefeller, **Jimmy Carter**, Richard Nixon, Dwight Eisenhower and all three Kennedy brothers. The CFR has also been accused of being yet another **Bavarian Illuminati** front organization, but because JFK was an alleged CFR member, how exactly that correlates with the Illuminati behind his **assassination** is the subject of some debate.

Cyber Privacy

"It keeps the Web from surfing you." These words are the punch line from the late-night, cable-TV commercial for a computer program called *Guard Dog* from Cybermedia. "The Internet may be your window on the world, but is it also the world's window on you?" That a company should be running commercials for a PC program that claims to ensure Internet privacy can only serve to demonstrate the depths of fear that many computer users experience regarding the idea that Big Brother may be monitoring their travels on the Web. **Internet karma**? In fact, many of these fears may to some degree be well founded. It is technically possible for any Web server to monitor its customer's movements and store the information. Many Web sites have the capacity to commit to memory the ID of anyone making a hit on the site. E-mail lists are bought and sold just like old-fashioned mailing lists. Where did you think all that spam comes from? As with all forms of mass surveillance, the stumbling block is the sheer volume of time when nothing is happening and the sheer volume of irrelevant information that has to be stored. As with phone tap paranoia, Big Brother just doesn't have the time to watch everyone, and fear is the true motivating force. If a program like *Guard Dog* makes you feel better, go for it. Peace of mind can be worth the shipping and handling.

Cyborg Man

Kevin Warwick, a professor of cybernetics at Reading University in England, has made the predictions of cyberpunk science fiction a slightly uncomfortable reality. Dubbed by the British press, "The Cyborg Man," he is the first human being—or at least the first human being who isn't a well-guarded military secret—to have a functioning microchip implanted in his body. "This is really the first step to establishing the communication link from computer to human inside the human body." The 3mm wide and 23mm long chip is in Warwick's left arm, just below the elbow. Currently, it opens doors for him, turns on lights when he enters a room, and records all of his daily movements around campus. Later though, he foresees that the chip's memory will also contain his Social Security number, his blood type, his banking information, and will replace his credit cards.

Warwick was also well aware that by receiving the implant he was running certain risks. Doctors warned that the implant might blow up inside his arm or disintegrate and start floating around his body. So far, so good however, and the only discomfort he has suffered is some soreness and bruising from the original surgical procedure, plus a certain odd emotional relationship to the device. "What I actually feel is not as though the machine is part of me or that I am part of the machine, but we are linked, we are connected by a physical link." He is, on the other hand, concerned about future dangers in this kind of implant usage and worries that governments could succumb to the temptation to use chip implants as means of control and repression.

Cycling

The news is bad for groupies at the Tour de France. According to Harin Padma-Nath, an assistant professor of urology at the University of South Carolina, excessive cycling—over 100 miles a week—may result in impotence. Repeated thrusting down on the pedals pounds the groin against the seat, damaging sexually critical arteries and nerves. The damage is irreversible, but—and here's the kicker—it may take some years to become noticeable.

D

DEA

When, in the 1989 Gus Van Sant film *Drugstore Cowboy*, William Burroughs delivers the line "drugs have been progressively scapegoated and demonized in this country as an excuse for the establishment of a global police force," audiences cheered. Uncle Bill was telling it like it was. And if you want to see a model for this planet-wide five-0, you need look no further than the federal Drug Enforcement Agency.

Since the collapse of the Soviet Union, the DEA may well have surpassed the **CIA**, if not the **NSA**, as the most insidious of all superpower intelligence/law-enforcement operations. From the moment the Berlin Wall came down, the DEA has busily promoted the idea that drugs are the natural successor to communism as the archdemon now loose upon the planet and that they, and only they, are the true soldiers of righteousness. In the late 1980s, the newspeak term "narco-terrorism" was coined in anticipation of the massive military operation staged by President George Bush that culminated in the invasion of Panama and the arrest of Manuel Noriega—according to Ted Koppel, "the biggest, one-man drug bust in history." Narco-terrorism seemed a little grandiose, even to the American media, and although Dan Rather favored it for awhile on the *CBS News*, it hardly caught on.

The fact that they may not have been able to sell America on their line didn't exactly deter the DEA. Although Bill Clinton proved to be a great deal less rabid than his immediate predecessors on the subject of drugs, the agency continues to go from strength to strength, taking on an increasingly global role. Far from being content with merely busting drug dealers and attempting to keep narcotics from entering the U.S., the DEA now involves itself in areas that were previously the strictly protected turf of the **CIA**. The agency plays a major role in the internal politics of Burma, Turkey, Columbia, Peru, Mexico, Bolivia, and many other countries with a reputation as drug producers. Under the guise of crop eradication, it maintains small private armies at various points around the world. On the economic front of the war on drugs, the purchase of poppy crops in the Southeast Asian Golden Triangle and of coca plantations in Bolivia and Peru, and massive involvement in drug buys in the U.S. and parts of Latin America quite possibly—and with a bizarre irony—make the DEA the largest single investor in the global narcotics industry.

At home, the DEA also moves in many strange territories. On one hand, it has infiltrated the medical profession, acting against doctors who, in its opinion, prescribe unorthodoxly large quantities of drugs to chronic-pain patients, and targeting other doctors who advocate the medicinal use of **marijuana**, even in states where such treatment is legal. At the same time, the agency is currently engaged in a quiet, but nonetheless extensive, media-control campaign to suppress even the discussion of the legalization or decriminalization of drugs. The easily observed knee-jerk reaction of the DEA, whenever the subject of legalization comes up, tends to suggest that it is exactly what the agency fears more than anything else. And why not? Without drug laws to enforce, the DEA would have to shut up shop and 100,000 narcs would be out of a job.

Or would they?

Some DEA watchers warn that to shut down the DEA might not be so easy. When Richard Nixon created the DEA from the old Federal Bureau of

Narcotics and Dangerous Drugs, he deliberately set it up with a quasi-corporate structure. In theory, the DEA has enough ongoing operations that actually turn a profit that trafficking could continue indefinitely without *any* federal funding. Of course, what exactly that hard core would do is a whole other matter.

Perhaps the major source of worry about the DEA should be that with its increasingly labyrinthine, cloak-and-dagger approach to drug enforcement, it could replace the AFT (personified in the ninja warriors at Ruby Ridge and Waco) as the extreme right's model of the sinister, out-of-control, federal agency going where it's not wanted, doing what's not required, and generally trampling underfoot the rights of citizens.

Death

A May 1997 CNN news report stated that women who were exposed to second-hand smoke ran a greater risk of death. Clearly, the headline was another case of the sloppy language that is so common in TV news. But in a wholly Freudian manner, it also pointed to a contemporary American piece of wishful thinking that death is somehow avoidable, or given the right medical treatment, or with sufficient healthcare spending, it can be delayed indefinitely. Sorry. We all die, friends and neighbors, and there's not a damn thing we can do about it.

Deathray

The Russians may have a deathray that they haven't used yet. That is the contention of retired U.S. Army Colonel Thomas E. Beardon, who claims that the former Soviet Union spent decades working on electro**magnetic** guns that operated on applications of the futuristic theories of **Nikola Tesla**. While the U.S. surged ahead in nuclear weaponry, the Soviets were concentrating their cutting-edge, ex-Nazi scientists on the creation of a raygun that employed phase conjugation and time distortion (TD) technology. The only problem is that a TD raygun tends to set off all nuclear missiles in a radius of about 500 miles and is therefore a very dubious proposition while nukes continue to abound. According to Beardon, this is why Mikhail Gorbachev jumped at **Ronald Reagan**'s Zero Option plan that called for the eventual elimination of all nuclear weapons. Once the H-bombs and A-bombs are all gone, Russia will dominate a helpless Earth with its TD deathray machines.

Deep Creek Lodge

Built on an abandoned Boy Scout camp in the woods of Maryland, Deep Creek Lodge has become a key location in the conspiracy theories surrounding the **CIA** and its various forms of mind-control experimentation. It was where, during the the CIA's **MKULTRA** LSD experiments, Dr. Sidney Gottleib and his MKULTRA researchers would conduct three-day brainstorming retreats with guests from other branches of the intelligence and experimental weapons communities. It was at one of these retreats that Army Chemical Corps scientist Frank Olson was spiked by Gottleib with the acid that would trigger his subsequent suicide and the scandal that followed it.

Other reports claim the Deep Creek Lodge was also used as a covert center for the training of child prostitutes for blackmail and other sexual entrapment operations. This was the charge brought by Claudia Mullens, an alleged survivor of these experiments, when she testified before the President's Advisory Committee on Radiation Experiments in March of 1995. Back in 1959 she had seemingly been an inmate at Deep Creek. "We were taught different ways to please men and at the same time get them to talk about themselves."

De-evolution

The equation is simple. For the most part, intelligent, enlightened, responsible people, aware of the critical human overpopulation of the planet, either have no children or limit their families to a small and manageable number of offspring. The ill-informed, benighted, or stupid place no limits on the number of children they have. What this amounts to is counter-Darwinism in action.

Already rumors circulate how, in the poorest barriadas of Rio de Janeiro, children are surviving to puberty with markedly reduced IQs, and even more disturbing, deathsquads of off-duty policemen hunt and kill these children on weekends.

Dixon, Illinois

Dixon, Illinois, the birthplace of **Ronald Reagan** and a possible candidate for the title, "Heart of the Conservative Heartland," has from 1996 onward, been plagued by a rash of UFO encounters.

Dolly

Dolly, the fully-grown sheep successfully cloned by researchers in Scotland and revealed to the public in 1997, heated up the simmering furor around the whole business of cloning and the possibility of cloning humans. Prompted by academic groups like the Bioethics Advisory Commission, President Bill Clinton immediately slapped a moratorium on all federal funding for human clone experiments and began moving to outlaw that kind of research entirely. Unfortunately, this would hardly deter anyone rich enough and megalomaniacal enough to want to get into *The Boys from Brazil* business and duplicate replicas of him or herself. To paraphrase the gun lobby—if clones are outlawed, only outlaws will be cloned. With Dolly, plus the cloned rhesus monkeys in the U.S. that went public later that year, the can of worms is seriously open and nothing will close it ever again.

Dreamland

Dreamland, or alternately D.R.E.A.M.Land, is an alternative name given to the highly secret government installation, **Area 51**, at Groom Lake, Nevada. The D.R.E.A.M initials stand for Data Repository and Electronic Amassing Management.

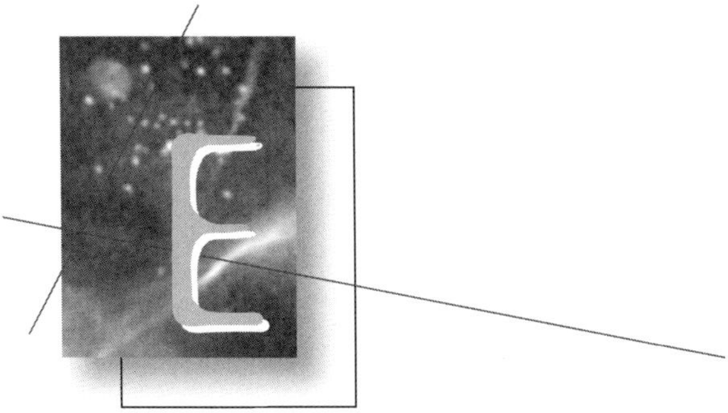

ECHELON

A recent report by the Civil Liberties Committee of the European Parliament revealed that the **CIA**, working in concert with the **National Security Agency** and British intelligence operations, routinely intercepts phone, fax, and e-mail transmissions all over the world. The same report revealed the existence of ECHELON, a part of the Anglo-American U.K./U.S. system of super computers. Through ECHELON, monitored transmissions are collected at a central hub in London and then sent by satellite to Fort Meade in Maryland via the Menwith Hill facility in Yorkshire, now the biggest spy station in the world. Unlike the older electronic spy systems developed during the Cold War that eavesdropped on purely military communications, ECHELON targets civilian governments, organizations, and businesses in every country. "The system works by indiscriminately intercepting very large quantities of communications and then siphoning out what is valuable by using artificial intelligence aids like MEMEX to find key words." The report concludes by bluntly advising, "The European Parliament should reject proposals from the United States to have private messages on the global communications network (the Internet) accessible to U.S. intelligence agencies."

Eco-Terrorists

This is a term coined during the **Reagan** administration to negatively describe groups and individuals, including Greenpeace and other similar organizations, who were prepared to resort to direct action to prevent the ongoing destruction of the environment. The invented word was test flown a number of times in the media but failed to catch the public imagination. Apparently, the hope that middle America would see the protection of whales or four hundred-year-old redwoods as the acts of dangerous sociopaths was unfounded, and the word was quietly dropped from the Republican spin-control lexicon.

Electric Chair, The

Today, even the staunchest supporters of capital punishment will agree that the electric chair as a means of execution is hardly the most efficient piece of machinery. "Old Sparky" is unreliable and cruelly painful. In many cases, a number of jolts have to be delivered to the condemned before he or she is finally dead. In most respects, if the state feels the need to execute felons, the gallows—which the electric chair replaced in many states—was a far more efficient device. The U.S. only has the electric chair as a result of a promo campaign by Thomas Edison that electricity was the "power of the future." Edison, willing to employ all and any possible gimmicks in boosting the idea of electricity, first sold the idea of an electric chair as the modern happening method of execution to the New York State prison authorities. The first execution took place at Sing Sing in 1891; the idea was quickly adopted by a number of other states, and has now remained with us for over a century.

The Eleven

From the depths of the rock 'n' roll sector of the extremely bizarre, stories surface of The Eleven, also known as The Eleven Committee, who, from their secret headquarters in California, operate as the ruling group of international Satanists. They have major ties with the Italian and U.S. Mafia, international banking, and the **Bavarian Illuminati**. The Eleven are also connected with the (former) Grateful Dead, Pink Floyd, the Eagles, and the Steve Miller Band, who, as this particular weird rumor has it, are all the propaganda arms of the global Satanist movement. Oddly, no one claims The Rolling Stones have any connection to all this Satanic majesty.

Element 115

In the April 1994 issue of *Omni*, Bob Lazar explains in an interview the functioning of the alien aircraft currently being studied inside **Area 51**, the ultra-secret base at Groom Lake in the Nevada desert. "The reactor is fueled with an element that is not found here on Earth. Part of my contribution to the program was to find out where this element plugged into the periodic chart. Well it didn't plug in anywhere, so we placed it at an atomic number of 115." Bob Lazar has been a controversial figure in the UFO conspiracy community since he emerged to prominence in the early 1990s, claiming he had been employed in reverse engineering alien craft at Area 51. Lazar insists that he was recruited and officially employed by the Department of Naval Intelligence, although the DNI denies any knowledge of him. He can, however, produce tax records in support of his claim, and his name appears on a bootlegged Area 51 employee phone directory.

"In all the discs at S4, there were three gravity amplifiers positioned in a triad at the base of the craft. These were the propulsion devices. Essentially, what they did was to amplify gravity waves out of phase with those of the Earth ...Element 115 is a stable element, but one with some interesting properties. It can be used inside the reactor as a fuel, but also as the source of an energy field accessed and amplified by the craft's gravity amplifiers." Lazar goes into more detail on the UFO propulsion system in a videocassette he markets himself. Unfortunately, parts of this quasi-scientific outline sound like the fictional matter/antimatter propulsion systems used on the TV series *Star Trek*.

Endangered Lions

The lions in South Africa's vast Kruger National Park are rapidly succumbing to an incurable form of tuberculosis in disastrous numbers. Park veterinarians, who have been testing lions in batches of thirty to thirty-five, have discovered in each batch that the number of those infected is in the high twenties. The more gloomy prognostications fear the entire population may be dead in little more than a couple of years. The African lion has no natural immunity to tuberculosis, and it is thought that the lions are catching the disease from infected African buffalo. The lion and the buffalo, however, occupied the same habitat for thousands of years without the problem occurring previously, and the mystery is why an epidemic should suddenly break out with such virulence.

F

Face on Mars, The

All kinds of theories have been proposed and explanations have been offered to account for the surface formation resembling a human face that showed up in the photographs taken by the NASA Viking I orbiter in 1976 as it passed over the area known as Cydonia in the northern hemisphere of the planet Mars. UFO pundit Richard C. Hoagland has all but made a career out of what he calls his "Intelligence Hypothesis," based on the face and the nearby formations that look like pyramids with five-sided bases. He uses them as evidence that intelligent life—capable of developing a fairly advanced level of civilization—once existed on Mars, possibly millions of years ago.

By far the strangest theory though, is the one presented by a number of **Elvis Presley** fans that the face on Mars is a huge, mountain-sized sculpture of the Elvis that proves he was an interplanetary entity, incarnated on different planets at different times. A version of the same idea did appear as a cover story in the September 20, 1988, edition of the tabloid weekly *Sun*, but only after it had circulated for some time among fans.

FEMA

In the perceptions of most Americans, the Federal Emergency Management Agency (FEMA) is looked on as a friend in need, the coordinating federal agency that moves in with damage control in the aftermath of any major disaster, fire, flood, hurricane, or earthquake. Along with charities like the Red Cross, it provides tents, food, water, fuel, and the other basics of mass life support. This, however, is not a view shared by the extreme right and the **militia** mindset, who seem unable to accept that even the slightest good can come out of Washington and the federal government. According to their major theorists and Internet propaganda mill, FEMA—under Executive Order 11490, signed into law by Richard Nixon in October 1969—in the event of a declared National State of Emergency, would have the power to suspend the Constitution and assume total control of the following:

- The communications media via the Emergency Broadcast System.
- All electrical power, petroleum, gas, fuels, and minerals.
- Food resources and farms.
- All modes of transportation, highways, railroads, seaports, airports, and aircraft.
- The mobilization of civilians into work brigades.
- The national registration of all civilians.
- Population relocation.

With all this power vested in FEMA, the rightists' scenario (not unlike the **REX 84** plan devised by Oliver North) makes the case that all it requires is the election of a president controlled by **The New World Order**. That president then finds a pretext to declare a national emergency—civil disorder, as in the case of the Los Angeles riots, would be a perfect excuse—and from that point on, FEMA would be in totalitarian control of the entire country. The Constitution would be history, as would all citizens' rights. Working with the 300th Military Police POW

Command based in Livonia, Michigan, a round-up would commence of all those designated as enemies of the state, identified from lists that are maintained right now on the computers at the **Mt. Weather** facility near Bluemont, Virginia, and constantly updated. Those arrested would be held in concentration camps, already prepared on federal land and existing military bases, while awaiting the ultimate disposition of their fate. At this point, the NWO troops and their **black helicopters** would move in and, for America, the fat lady would have sung.

Foo Fighters

Foo fighters was the term used during World War II for the mysterious fireballs that were regularly sighted shadowing Allied aircraft, particularly the huge formations of Flying Fortresses conducting daylight bombing raids on Germany. The fear was that these might be **Nazi flying saucers**, some kind of unmanned experimental weapon that the Luftwaffe was in the process of testing. This triggered the very first U.S. investigations of the phenomenon of unidentified flying objects that preceded Bluebook, Grudge, Sign, and all the other Air Force UFO study projects with their fancy code names and less-than-plausible explanations.

Four-Twenty

The term "four-twenty" was first picked up by the mass media in the aftermath of the April 1999 mass killings at Columbine High School, in Littleton, Colorado. Because the two armed outsiders, Eric Harris and Dylan Klebold, who planned and conducted this **high school slaughter**, exhibited a fascination with Nazi regalia and maybe actual Nazism, and because the figures "4-20" turned up repeatedly on their Web sites and in other left-behind effects, the immediate assumption was that the numbers referred to the birthdate of Adolf Hitler—April 20, 1889—and that the Littleton massacre was a remembrance of the Fuhrer's 110th birthday. It was a fast and easily manageable conclusion, but like so many media conclusions, perhaps somewhat off its mark.

The idea of the Hitler connection was quickly refuted by stoners, Deadheads, and other members of the recreational **marijuana** subculture, who pointed out that four-twenty had been around in the dope-smoking community for many years and was used as a general euphemism for pot smoking, or more specifically, as a term for firing up the first joint of the day. Its origins are a little hazy and have been debated at length in the marijuana magazine *High Times*. Some claim it was a now-abandoned California police radio code indicating "marijuana smoking in process," that it was a CB-radio truck drivers call that a driver was high on reefer, or that it was the average time of day when a high school stoner would be out of school and ready to light up. This, however, was never mentioned in stories about the Littleton massacre in the mainstream media—maybe because the concept of teen neo-Nazis was simpler to comprehend than that of dope-smoking armed malcontents dressed up like the James Gang, engaging in random suicide raids. Maybe CNN never checks its facts with stoned neo-hippies.

Freemasons

It would take a small library to completely chronicle the world history of Freemasonry. If its own legends are to be believed, the Freemasons are the world's oldest secret society and have been surrounded by conspiracy theories dating back thousands of years. The origins of Freemasonry, according to some accounts, go back to before the biblical flood, to the three sons of Lamach, a contemporary of Noah. One discovered geometry, a second was the first Mason, and the third was the first blacksmith. Others place it as beginning with the building of the Temple of Solomon in Jerusalem and suggest that much of Masonic occult mysticism was symbolically embodied into the architecture of the Temple. One set of historians takes a slightly less dramatic view, stating that a form of Freemasonry first evolved out of the craft guilds of medieval Europe. These were formed, not unlike early trade unions, during the construction of the great Gothic cathedrals and immediately came into conflict with the church in what was nothing more than an employer-employee context that was the start of their bad rap for being secretive and threatening. Another historical theory, however, is that Freemasonry was a cover for the continuing secret practice of ancient pagan religions during the periods of church power and persecution that culminated in the Inquisition. A third school of thought claims that much of Freemasonry as we know it today can be traced to the eighteenth-century revival of interest in paganism and the occult.

Whatever the truth of the antecedents of Freemasonry—and if one thing can be said about the Masons, it's that they sure know how to keep their secrets—they were never particularly popular with the rest of the world. Monarchs have always looked upon them as dangerously independent and republican. The established church has viewed them as hostile, uncontrollable, and possibly Satanic. The average guy in the street has traditionally regarded the members of local Masonic lodges and temples as a privileged elite with a perverse taste for bizarre costumes and strange, if not absurd, rituals. The fact that the Masons have included among their numbers a high percentage of judges, police officers, politicians, and prominent businessmen always created the impression that they gave and received preferential treatment from each other in business and within the judicial system. This has made them a target for a great deal of outsider prejudice and resentment. In Victorian London, for example, it didn't take much for popular paranoia to make a Masonic connection to the Jack the Ripper murders in the 1890s. Stalin outlawed Freemasonry and executed prominent Masons. Hitler did much the same, although not before he'd borrowed heavily from Masonic ideas and symbols for the occult core of Nazism.

Prior to World War II, Freemasons loomed large in the quasi-fantasy world of secrets and conspiracy. But in the second half of the twentieth century, their power to conjure angry images of control by stealth and manipulation has been largely usurped by fear of the intelligence community in its various forms. Since the 1970s, the **Bavarian Illuminati** has taken over the all-powerful and almost demonic role once held by the Masons, who are now primarily seen as yet another old boy's club, carving up the town or city's business and politics from behind firmly closed doors.

G

Gates, Bill

As if to prove that nobody likes a multi-billionaire, the following theory began to circulate on the Internet in the spring of 1999. Bill Gates, the overlord of the giant Microsoft computer software empire, who now has an annual income larger than a medium-sized country, is in fact, the **Antichrist**. The logic of this decidedly odd pronouncement is based on the idea that if you take the letters of Gates' full name—William Henry Gates III—and express it numerically in the computer code ASCII (American Standard Code for Information Interchange), the resulting numbers add up to 666, and that is, as we all know, the number of the Great Beast in **The Book of Revelation**.

Gehlen, Reinhard

Although it may not be strictly true—and it certainly lets a lot of others off the hook of responsibility for their actions—much of the shadow-world horror of the last half-century can at least be partially blamed on Reinhard Gehlen. And why not? Isn't it always good to have a convenient Nazi to take the rap? Gehlen was Hitler's chief of intelligence on the eastern front during the latter stages of World War II. His power took a quantum leap after the failed "Night of the Generals" bomb plot and coup in 1944, after which the SS took total control of both military and civilian government in Nazi Germany. At the same time, seeing that the war was lost on the chessboard, and it was only a matter of time and body count before the Allies reached Berlin, Gehlen and Martin Borman, his patron in the Nazi hierarchy, secretly began to prepare for defeat. Without the knowledge of Hitler, Gehlen laid the foundations of the Odessa organization, which provided escape routes to South America, the Middle East, Canada, and the U.S. for hundreds of SS war criminals.

Gehlen went considerably further, however, than merely organizing the escape of upper echelons of Nazism when the ultimate collapse came. As the controller of Nazi intelligence operations during the final stages of the war, he not only had agents all over Eastern Europe who remained in place even after the Red Army rolled over their areas of operation, but also had pipelines into the Pentagon. He used these contacts to propose, even before Germany had formally surrendered, a highly secret but very tempting offer. If the U.S. forces of occupation in Germany granted him and his people immunity from war crimes prosecutions and allowed him to keep his former Nazi spynet intact, he would supply the U.S. with otherwise unobtainable intelligence from inside the countries occupied by the Soviet Union. Gehlen had correctly judged that, within months of conquering Germany from the east and west, the Soviets and the U.S. and its allies would start regarding each other as the new enemy.

The OSS, the U.S. wartime intelligence operation that preceded the **Central Intelligence Agency**, shamelessly jumped at the offer. According to researcher Carl Oglesby, this deal with the devil was consummated during the course of two months of top-secret negotiations at Fort Hunt near Washington. By the spring of 1946, Gehlen was back in business, spying on the Russians with several thousand of his former Nazi colleagues. Hundreds of other SS and Gestapo intelligence agents and Nazi scientists and technicians were also secretly relocated in the U.S. under the auspices of the OSS program code-named "Operation Paperclip."

When, in 1947, the OSS was disbanded and the CIA established to take its place, a hard spine of its field agents and technical advisors were Gehlen's people. Although they now presented themselves as dedicated anti-Communists, many were only barely reformed Nazis, and in the opinion of many CIA critics, their mindset did a lot to establish the methods and attitudes of the agency and may have been responsible for many of the moral ambiguities of future CIA operations.

GIGO

"Garbage In, Garbage Out." This maxim has to be the great caveat of the computer age. Frequently, when an individual or organization wants to blind we the people with state-of-the-art science, he, she, or it will parade a computer analysis or a computer simulation as means of verification and reinforcement. The idea is that Joe and Jane Q. Public are supposed to be so intimidated by computer infallibility that they will instantly buy the presented argument without question. The technique has been used in a variety of situations, ranging from the O. J. Simpson criminal trial to Gerald Pozner's defense of the Warren Commission in his book *Case Closed: Lee Harvey Oswald and the Assassination of JFK*. It must be remembered, however, that anything a computer may provide for us is only as good as the information that is fed to it in the first place. If inaccurate or deliberately misleading information is programmed in, inaccurate and misleading conclusions will come out. The other side of the same computer coin is the announcement that you can't have or do what you want because "our systems are down."

Gleason, Jackie

A not often heard story about Jackie Gleason is that the TV pioneer and star of *The Honeymooners*—frequently referred to in show business circles as "The Great One"—was also a serious student of UFO phenomena.

He named his residence in Peekskill, New York, "The Mothership" and designed it to resemble a flying saucer. An even stranger tale comes from his second wife, Beverly McKittrick. Apparently, one night in 1973, Gleason returned home looking visibly shaken. He told McKittrick an amazing story. With security clearance from no less than his martini pal and poker buddy Richard Nixon, he had just paid a visit to Homestead Air Force Base in Florida. He had been allowed to inspect a top-secret repository where the bodies of dead aliens from a number of UFO crashes were stored in refrigerated containers. Puts a new twist on "to the moon, Alice," doesn't it?

Glenn, John

On October 29, 1998, veteran astronaut and Ohio senator John Glenn became, at age seventy-seven, the oldest human being to travel in space when he joined the crew of the NASA shuttle mission STS-95. The event also gave rise to the bizarre rumor, in the form of Internet postings and radio call-ins to The Howard Stern Show, that the real reason the first American to orbit the Earth had returned to space was as a human representative—perhaps an ambassador from **Majestic 12**—summoned to attend an off-world meeting with the all-controlling grey aliens.

Global Corruption

As free-market capitalism extends and expands at unprecedented speed in the wake of the collapse of communism and the end of the Cold War, a new menace is perceived as, if not rearing its ugly head, at least casting a long shadow. Investors and money market managers are increasingly concerned that economic corruption could reach epidemic proportions and lay the groundwork for all kinds of world-scale financial disasters in the first half of the twenty-first century. A German-based study group called Transparency International is warning that the number of countries where little can be done without large-scale bribery is markedly on the increase. Organizations like the major international banks and the International Monetary Fund are continuing to make loans to nations where a risk exists of the current leaders simply stealing the national treasury as General Mobutu did in the former Zaïre.

In the fall of 1998, Transparency International prepared a chart that rated all the nations of the world according to their ongoing levels of internal corruption and potential for corruption in the future. Denmark emerged as the most honest country on Earth, followed by Finland, Sweden, New Zealand, and Canada. The U.S. came in at number seventeen, having slipped one position since a previous survey. Cameroon appears to be the most corrupt place on the planet but is closely challenged by Paraguay, Honduras, Tanzania, and Nigeria.

The Golden Rule

"The Golden Rule—Those with gold rule!"—graffiti in New York City.

Goldwater, Barry

Senator Barry Goldwater, the ultra-conservative who ran against Lyndon Johnson in the 1964 presidential election, was an experienced pilot who held the rank of general in the United States Air Force. He allegedly told the following story when the subject of UFOs came up. While en route to California in the early 1960s, he stopped off at Wright Patterson Air Base to visit his friend, Gen. Curtis LeMay, who would later command the air war in Vietnam. Goldwater had heard rumors of something known as the "Blue Room," where UFO artifacts and photographs—and according to some accounts, alien bodies—were kept. When he asked LeMay whether he could see it, the senator was more than a little shocked by his friend's almost violent response: "Hell, no. I can't go, you can't go, and don't ever ask again."

Goofy

"If Mickey's a mouse and Pluto's a dog, then what the hell is Goofy?"—Stephen King, *Stand By Me*.

Grand Rapids, Colorado

Since as early as 1917, the city of Grand Rapids, Colorado has, for no reason that anyone can fathom, been an epicenter for UFO sightings. The appearance of objects in the skies over Grand Rapids predates the first media flying saucer flaps in the 1940s and early 1950s, and through the 1990s, the sky traffic has become close to out-of-hand with residents reporting almost daily sightings of everything from small discs to large cylindrical motherships.

H

Hammer of Witches

Believe it or not, as Mr. Ripley used to say, prior to the late fifteenth century the Catholic Church took a fairly benign view of witchcraft and in no way associated it with the evils of Satanism. It was merely seen as a few ignorant peasants under the delusion they were worshipping pagan gods. All this changed in 1486 when a couple of Dominican monks, Heinrich Kramer and James Sprengler, decided that all this tolerance simply couldn't be tolerated. In their book, *Malleus Maleficarum,* also known as *Hammer of Witches*, Kramer and Sprengler advanced the doctrine that, far from being harmless rustic nonsense, witchcraft was "a diabolical heresy, which conspired to overthrow the Church and establish the kingdom of Satan on Earth." Pope Innocent VIII read their work and liked what he saw, immediately issuing a Papal bull condemning witches and plunging Europe into a 250-year bloodbath. Tens of millions of people—by far the majority being women—were tortured and executed in the name of rooting out the Devil and his works. As in all holocausts, scores were settled under the guise of religious hysteria, lands and fortunes were seized, and both the Church and private individuals reaped vast material rewards.

Usually a little leery about the works of the Papacy, the Protestant churches that had recently emerged from the Reformation were quick to steal the ideas of Kramer and Sprengler, adopt them as their own, and ruthlessly go about the Lord's business of hanging and burning. The same ideas were carried to America by the Pilgrims and manifested themselves in the horror trials at Salem and other Puritan witch-hunts. Since that time, the ideas contained in the *Malleus Maleficarum* have never really gone away, just lain dormant. Every so often, a new witchcraft/Satan cult scare erupts. In the case of the Moral Majority freak-out in the mid-1980s, for example, Pat Robertson and group of not-so-famous but equally opportunistic fundamentalists decided that, in the conservative heyday of the **Reagan** era, a well-organized network of Satanic cults had spread all across America. The claim was that they had infiltrated the school systems, were corrupting the kids with hypnotic suggestions recorded backward on heavy metal albums, and conducting thousands of human ritual sacrifices.

Fortunately, these modern witch-hunts have been a matter of trial by tabloid television and dubious hypnotic regression treatment rather than the rack and the thumbscrew. They quickly started to look a little absurd to all but the ideologically demented with their claims that Ozzy Osbourne was an agent of the **Antichrist**. An FBI spokesman was very clear that the Bureau (being no stranger to witch-hunts) took a fairly skeptical stand on Satanic cults. As far as the FBI was concerned, Satanic cults do exist, usually comprised of groups of disturbed teenagers or used as a cover for group sex activities. Now and then a murder is reported, but as far as mass human sacrifice is concerned, "we surely would have found at least a percentage of the bodies."

Hanta Virus

Although biological warfare research was outlawed by Richard Nixon in 1969, a loophole in the presidential order allowed for "purely defensive" bio-warfare research to continue. One virus that qualified for defensive research was the hanta virus. It was thought to have caused outbreaks of Korean hemorrhagic fever, which killed some 400 GIs during the Korean War, and was suspected of having been deliberately spread by the North Koreans or the Chinese via infected rodents. The hanta virus was shown to be responsible for supposedly unrelated outbreaks of an often fatal, flu-like illness in the Four Corners area of the southwestern United States in 1992 and subsequently spread to Texas, Nevada, and California. Critics of bio-warfare research pointed fingers at so-called "defensive" work that was being done on the virus, particularly as the first outbreaks were supposed to have occurred relatively close to Ford Wingate, where bio-warfare research was allegedly conducted, or at the very least, biological agents were stored.

An article in the June 1993 issue of *Science Magazine* stated categorically that military work on the virus ceased around 1990, having failed to show any practical results, and that around the same time, Fort Wingate had been closed, although it might continue to be a weapons research storage area. One researcher even publicly regretted that the Army had ceased work on the hanta virus because, in view of the Four Corners outbreak, continued bio-warfare research might have provided an avenue to a vaccine. Despite this and other public statements, Pentagon watchers remain less than convinced that the current hanta infections were not the result of an accidental release of the virus from Fort Wingate or some other government biotech facility. More sinister still was the theory that the release was deliberate, a clandestine test on the local population of Four Corners, the majority of whom are Navajo.

Harrelson, Charles Voyd

Charles Harrelson, self-confessed organized crime hit man, is the father of Woody Harrelson, star of TV's *Cheers* and movies that include *White Men Can't Jump*, *Natural Born Killers*, and *The People vs. Larry Flynt*. Harrelson has played a part, as one of the alleged shooters in Dealey Plaza, in a number of **JFK assassination** scenarios. Harrelson, who is currently serving a life term in the Marion Federal Penitentiary in Marion, Illinois, for the 1979 contract murder of U.S. District Judge John H. Wood Jr., at one point actually claimed that he was one of the marksmen on the grassy knoll. The only problem was that this confession was made by Harrelson, high on cocaine, holding a .44 magnum to his own head, and it came at the climax of a six-hour standoff with police. The incident had begun when Harrelson decided that the Corvette he was driving was making too much noise, and he shot it full of holes on the open highway.

Later, he would deny he had any hand in the Kennedy killing, telling British filmmaker Nigel Turner "On November 22nd, 1963, at 12:30, I was having lunch with a friend in a restaurant in Houston, Texas." The case of Harrelson is further complicated by the researchers working for columnist Jack Anderson who contended that Harrelson is one of the three "tramps" photographed minutes after the assassination in the railroad yards adjoining Dealey Plaza.

In an interview with Barbara Walters following the 1997 Academy Awards show, Woody Harrelson denied that his father was a part of any Kennedy conspiracy, but confirmed that he was a professional hit man, and volunteered the information that Harrelson Sr. had been trained to kill by the **CIA**.

Heaven's Gate

A paper from the Heaven's Gate manifesto titled "Our Position Against Suicide" was published on the cult's Web site a matter of days before their mass suicide:

> We fully desire, expect, and look forward to boarding a spacecraft from the Next Level very soon (in our physical bodies). There is no doubt in our mind that our being "picked up" is inevitable in the near future. But what happens between now and then is the big question. We are keenly aware of several possibilities.

> It could happen before the spaceship comes, one or more of us could lose our physical vehicles (bodies) due to "recall," accident, or at the hands of some irate individual. We do not anticipate this, but it is possible. Another possibility is that because of the position we take in our information, we could find so much disfavor with the powers that control this world that there could be attempts to incarcerate us or to subject us to some sort of psychological or physical torture. (Such was the case at Ruby Ridge or Waco.)
>
> It has always been our way to examine all possibilities and be mentally prepared for whatever may come our way. For example, consider what happened at Masada around 73 A.D. A devout Jewish sect, after holding out against a siege by the Romans to the best of their ability, and seeing that the murder, rape, and torture of their community was inevitable, determined that it was permissible for them to evacuate by a more dignified and less agonizing method. We have thoroughly discussed this topic (of willful exit of the body under such conditions), and have mentally prepared ourselves for this possibility (as can be seen in a few of our statements). However, this act certainly does not need serious consideration at this time and hopefully not in the future.

Sometime over the next few days, the Heaven's Gate people must have rethought their position and reached for the vodka, juice, and strychnine.

Hello Kitty

The Hello Kitty symbol can be seen all over Japan on T-shirts, lunch boxes, pen and pencil sets, and the entire gamut of small-ticket consumer goods. Akin to the U.S. "happy face," it is the face of a highly simplified cat with two pointy ears, two eyes, but—strangely—no mouth, and is marketed to millions of Japanese schoolgirls. Some believe it is merely a uniquely Japanese version of the happy face, but others claim it is the secret sign of a conspiracy of very young girls to overthrow their male-dominated society.

Hemp

The popular supposition has always been that the laws against **marijuana** continue to be enforced to protect the mental and physical health of the population and as a social-control measure similar to alcohol prohibition during the 1920s. An increasing body of evidence amassed over the last decade, although admittedly circumstantial, suggests that marijuana is outlawed as a result of a scheme perpetrated by William Randolph Hearst and the Du Pont corporation on the U.S. government and the governments of other countries.

Although smoking the leaves of the hemp plant (*cannabis sativa*) is a well-known and often demonized intoxicant, the rest of the plant, particularly the stems, have been used by man for thousands of years. Hemp fibers were woven into tough and durable ropes, high-quality paper, and hard-wearing fabrics used for everything from clothing to the sails of clipper ships and men o' war. Hemp oil is also a lubricant and a potential fuel, superior to many petroleum products. Hemp even figures prominently in U.S. history. Both George Washington and Thomas Jefferson cultivated it as a cash crop, and Mary Todd Lincoln came from a prosperous hemp growing family. The Declaration of Independence was written on hemp paper. The first flags were made from hemp cloth, as were the earliest Levis, and the canvas on the pioneers' covered wagons was also made from the plant's fibers.

The panic over marijuana—reefer madness, so to speak—was largely started in the early 1930s, primarily by newspaper baron William Randolph Hearst and Harry J. Anslinger, the head of the newly formed Federal Bureau of Narcotics. At the same time as Hearst and Anslinger whipped up public hysteria by blasting the "demon weed," a technical development was perfected that made the processing of hemp fibers considerably cheaper. So cheap in fact, that hemp would have undercut wood pulp as the most economic source of newsprint. The event of cheap hemp paper would have quite literally ruined the Hearst empire, which had massive timber and logging holdings. Another mega-corporation that would have been ruinously hurt by the new cheap hemp process was Du Pont, which had invested millions in research on cheap, man-made fibers like nylon and rayon, to which low-priced hemp would have also presented a potentially disastrous challenge.

Despite the anti-marijuana frenzy created by the Hearst press, Congress wasn't immediately stampeded into criminalizing hemp production. In 1930 the Siler Commission found the drug relatively harmless and recommended no criminal penalties be imposed. The American Medical Association came to a similar conclusion, but Anslinger used his considerable political clout to suppress these findings, and hemp was made effectively illegal all across the U.S. in 1937. Just to underscore the apparent spuriousness of this criminalization, the laws against hemp were repealed briefly during World War II when, due to the Japanese occupation of the Philippines—the only source of legal hemp—the U.S. Navy suffered a shortage of good quality rope. Once the crisis was over, though, the law was put back on the books.

Even though hemp could today provide a source of alternative fibers, pharmaceuticals, and lubricants, as well as a solution to deforestation and fossil fuel depletion, the Hearst-Anslinger mindset continues. Hemp is not used industrially, and thousands of otherwise law-abiding citizens are jailed under state or federal hemp/marijuana laws.

Hermaphrodite Cattle

In France, Holland, and the United Kingdom, the unsubstantiated story repeatedly circulates that genetic engineers have perfected a strain of hermaphrodite cattle that can inseminate themselves and have developed beyond the need for two genders.

High School Slaughter

Between October 1, 1997, and the spring of 1999 (the time of publication of this book), no fewer than seven fatal shooting incidents have taken place in high schools across the U.S. (In all but one of the cases, the culprits are unnamed since they are legally minors and may also be involved in continuing court hearings.) They are as follows:

October 1, 1997—A sixteen-year-old boy in Pearl, Mississippi, was accused of killing his mother and then going to his school and shooting nine students, two fatally. He has since been sentenced to life in jail. A second teen, alleged to have been the instigator of the murders, is still awaiting trial at the time of this writing. Both boys reputedly belonged to a cult-like group.

December 1, 1997—Three students were killed and five more wounded in a hallway at Heath High School in West Paduca, Kentucky. A boy of fourteen pleaded guilty but mentally ill and is serving life in prison. When asked why he did it, he said he "didn't know."

March 24, 1998—Four girls and a teacher were shot to death and ten more individuals wounded during a false fire alarm at a school in Jonesboro, Arkansas, when two boys, eleven and thirteen, opened fire from the woods. No motive was ever discovered, and the suspects have been convicted of murder in a juvenile court and can be held until they are twenty-one.

April 24, 1998—In Edinboro, Pennsylvania, a science teacher was shot to death by a fourteen-year-old student at an eighth-grade dance. The alleged shooter still awaits trial.

May 19, 1998—Three days before his graduation, an eighteen-year-old honor student shot dead a classmate who was dating his ex-girlfriend. The shooting took place on the parking lot of a high school in Fayetteville, Tennessee. He also awaits trial.

May 21, 1998—A fifteen-year-old boy opened fire at a high school in Springfield, Oregon, killing two teenagers and wounding twenty more. At home, he had already killed his parents. On a police videotape, he was asked why he felt the need to kill. His chillingly simple, yet inexplicable answer was "I had no other choice."

April 20, 1999—The slaughter reached a new height when members of **The Trenchcoat Mafia**, Eric Harris and Dylan Klebold, armed with pipe bombs and automatic weapons, attacked Columbine High School in the Denver suburb of Littleton, Colorado, with almost Vietcong suicide precision, killing sixteen and wounding dozens more. Although both Harris and Klebold killed themselves at the culmination of their "mission," friends tell how constant harassment by jock athletes pushed them first into an alienated fantasy world of goth music and Nazi fixations, and then finally drove them to a homicidal breaking point.

The religious right maintains that this is all a direct result of either Bill Clinton being elected to a second term as president or the outlawing of prayer in U.S. schools. An alternative theory is that the outbreaks of gun violence are, in fact, a direct descendant of the rash of killings that took place in the mail-sorting offices of the U. S. Postal Service in the late 80s. At that time, rumors abounded that killer postal workers were being driven to violent homicide as a result of postal facilities being secretly used by various Federal intelligence agencies for **MKULTRA**-style, behavior modification experiments. The current outbreak of speculation is that the focus of these experiments—working on the "get 'em while they're young" principle—has now shifted to high schools across America.

Hill, Betty and Barney

Betty and Barney Hill earned their place in the weird history of the twentieth century by being the first Americans to go on public record as suffering **abduction by aliens**. On the night of September 19, 1961, the Hills, a respectable and sober married couple, "lost" two hours while returning to their home in New Hampshire from a holiday in Canada. After two years, during which Barney suffered from chronic insomnia and Betty was plagued by nightmares, they went to Boston psychiatrist Dr. Benjamin Simon. Under hypnosis, both the Hills revealed that in the course of the drive, they had been "flagged down by small, grey humanoid beings with unusual eyes" and taken into some kind of glowing craft. They were subjected to various medical-style tests, and skin, hair, and sperm samples were taken, inadvertently setting the standard pattern for the vast majority of alien abduction stories that would follow. Although Dr. Simon never claimed to believe it was a genuine abduction, but thought the couple had somehow experienced an odd "shared dream," their story was made into a 1975 film, *The UFO Incident*, with James Earl Jones playing Barney. The film assumed their story was real.

One slightly disturbing factor in the Hill's case is that when debunkers attempt to disprove their abduction claim, the fact that they were an interracial couple always seems to be used as a reason for them to be more likely to share hallucinations or otherwise behave oddly.

Hitler's Assassination

In the summer of 1998, the British Public Records Office released a large quantity of previously classified papers from latter stages of World War II. One set of documents related directly to the activities of the German section of the highly secret Special Operations Executive (SOE), led by Major Field-Robertson. It specialized in all manner of dirty tricks intended to create problems for the Nazi leadership, including disinformation and assassination. The documents, eagerly pawed through by delighted historians, journalists, and sensation seekers, revealed that much of the SOE's efforts remained on the prank level. They included operations like feeding the German people lurid rumors about the sex lives of the Nazi elite, and even circulating forged stamps on which Hitler's portrait had been replaced by that of SS chief Heinrich Himmler. (These were supposed to create suspicions that the SS were planning to oust the Fuhrer and completely take over the government of Germany.) Somewhat more serious was a well-developed SOE plot to assassinate Adolf Hitler in the fall of 1944. Had this scheme succeeded, it could have ended the war early, saved millions of lives, halted the Final Solution, and meant that the Iron Curtain would have fallen much further to the east. Why then, after exhaustive research and planning and the full approval of British Prime Minister Winston Churchill, was the plan mysteriously cancelled?

An SOE memo dated October 17, 1944, shows that the assassination plot, code-named Operation Foxley, was all but set to go. Following the failed "Night of the Generals" bomb plot against Hitler in the summer of that year, the British had decided to take the initiative. At first, the proposals had been outlandish verging on ludicrous, equally silly as some of the **CIA** plots to kill **Fidel Castro** twenty years later. Early brainstorming came up with suggestions like poisoning Hitler's milk, infecting his clothing with deadly bacteria, or finishing him with a toxic fountain pen. Eventually, Foxley was narrowed down to one eminently more sensible scenario. SOE concluded that Hitler was most vulnerable when he was at the Berghof, his mountain retreat in Bavaria, and could be taken out by a "first-class marksman" using a Mauser rifle with a telescopic sight. A shooter, Captain E.H. Bennett, a British military attaché in Washington, was selected and, by way of backup, a Special Air Service (SAS) team would be parachuted in to blow up Hitler's car with PIAT anti-tank rockets when he sped to safety after a near miss by the primary sniper.

It was decided that the best chance of success would be by making the hit on Hitler when he took his morning walk. The Fuhrer was a stickler for routine and, literally come rain or shine, he would take a fifteen- to twenty-minute stroll on the grounds of the Berghof between 10 and 11 A.M. It was also more than possible that Hitler would present Bennett with a clear shot. He hated being crowded by his guards and had reportedly yelled at one SS man who was walking too closely "If you're frightened, go and guard yourself."

With all this in place, the sudden turnaround and quiet shelving of the plan seems close to inexplicable. A possible explanation was offered by journalist Robert Harris, writing in the London *Daily Mail*, just after the release of the SOE documents. He suggested that Field-Robertson had backed off from the idea of an assassination because he feared that it might turn the Nazi leader into a martyr and create "a whole new generation of scapegoats." Harris pointed out that after World War I, Hitler had come to power by promoting the fiction that Germany had lost the war only after being stabbed in the back by the Jews and socialists. Had he been killed by the British, power would have been transferred to a caretaker government that would have most likely negotiated a swift surrender. In this situation, it might have been all too possible for the German people to be manipulated into wondering "what if?" The Nazis not only had to be defeated but clearly seen to be defeated to ensure a lasting peace. Official British reasoning appears to have been that World War II could only be brought to proper closure by the capture of Hitler or his death at his own hand—as would, in fact, happen. Whether or not this was the correct analysis, the Hitler assassination plot was allowed to hang dormant until April 1945 when, with the Russians in Berlin and Hitler just days away from shooting himself, it was officially abandoned.

HIV

Perhaps the greatest gauge of the distrust of government among large sections of the population is the perpetuation of the rumor that a combination of the **CIA**, **NSA**, and the Army Chemical Corps Special Operations Division (SOD) at Fort Detrick, Maryland, designed, developed, and then set loose the HIV virus on an unsuspecting planet. For over a decade the tale has circulated among black activists, gay militants, and conspiracy buffs. It should be profoundly hoped that in actuality there is no truth in the story. If there were, it would certainly qualify as the worst atrocity in world history, eclipsing even the Nazi death camps.

The core of supposed reality in the AIDS story is an alleged budget appropriation, passed by the U.S. Congress in 1969 as part of House Bill 15090. HB 15090 apparently included $10 million for, as subsequent Senate Committee testimony is supposed to have revealed, the production of "a synthetic biological agent for which no natural immunity could have been acquired...a new infective microorganism which could differ in certain important aspects from any known disease-carrying organisms. Most important of these is that it might be refractory to the immunological and therapeutic processes upon which we depend to maintain our relative freedom from infectious disease." The development of this bacterial weapon could plainly do nothing other than create a prolonged and deadly pandemic.

Because no hard evidence seems to exist beyond this point, the speculation takes off from there. According to the published theories, the ultimate use of the bacteria was to depopulate Africa, leaving its vast land area and underlying natural resources open for exploitation by Western corporations. Initially, however, the field tests of the man-made and sexually transmitted epidemic were to be made on "undesirable sections of the domestic population." Blacks, gays, and Hispanics were specifically targeted. The U.S. testing was carried out by agents working under the cover of a hepatitis B research program supposedly conducted by the Centers for Disease Control, in New York, San Francisco, and four other U.S. cities. Once these were complete, the virus was introduced into Africa by a smallpox immunization program operated by the World Health Organization.

Again, at this point, we have to make it clear that no satisfactory hard evidence can be produced linking AIDS to a conspiracy. The fact does remain that AIDS is currently ravaging Africa, and to quote epidemic specialist Dr. Robert Strecker, "without a cure, the entire black population of Africa will be dead within fifteen years. Some countries are beyond epidemic status."

Hollow Earth Theory

Essentially very Victorian, and straight from the pages of an Edgar Rice Burroughs Tarzan novel, the Hollow Earth Theory is a concept that still surfaces now and again. The Earth is supposedly hollow, lit by some kind of heated core, and life and even civilization thrive there. According to one piece of folklore, explorer Admiral Richard Byrd located a huge chasm that provided access to the hollow Earth during his 1926 flight over the North Pole, but the discovery was kept from the public. Further hollow Earth stories claim that the Nazis spent considerable effort attempting to locate the entrance to the hollow Earth. Some even go so far as to assert that they actually found it and that the **Nazi flying saucers** operate from there. These third-generation Nazis are in league with the Naga, a race of "serpent people" who live in a subterranean continent beneath the Himalayas and are evolutionary descendants of the dinosaurs that escaped underground during the "Great Cataclysm." The Naga hate humans with a vile passion and wish, through their network of human thralls and dupes, to turn the surface of the Earth into the perfect lizard environment. Hence pollution, the greenhouse effect, and global warming.

Hoover, J. Edgar

It was revealed after his death that J. Edgar Hoover—the first director of the FBI, who for half a century ruled at times what seemed to be an American Gestapo—was a homosexual and transvestite in private. Poet Allen Ginsberg was one of the few to make the following kind of comment: "I haven't seen anybody discussing the consequences of J. Edgar Hoover being a closeted queen aside from the hee haw, the joke that he was a transvestite at times. He was the acme and icon of the right-wing, sourpuss sector of the population, and all of a sudden it turns out that he was a complete hypocrite. I haven't seen anybody discuss the social consequences."

Hot Guns, Hotter Gals

A mail-order catalog from a military and survivalist paraphernalia operation called Delta Press in El Dorado, Arizona, says it all in a blurb about a videocassette titled *Rock & Roll #3—Hot Guns, Hotter Gals*, offered for $59.95. "You've got to see this tape to believe it. Fourteen outrageous, sexy girls in *string bikinis* and high heels blast away with the hottest full auto machine guns ever produced. Professionally produced like the MAC-10, Uzi, M-16, AK-47 and MP-5. You'll love every action-packed minute. Approximate running time: sixty minutes."

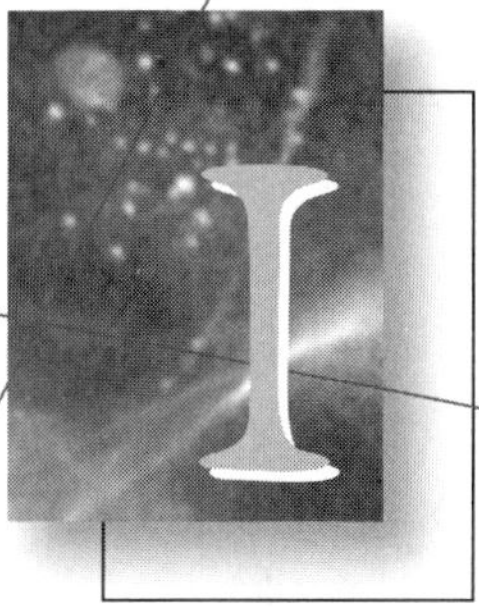

Icebergs

While meteorologists and geophysicists are unable to resolve the debate over whether global warming is really happening—and if so, how fast—huge chunks are breaking off Antarctica and floating north into warmer waters. In the summer of 1998, an iceberg thirty-five miles long, about twelve miles wide, and weighing about 750 billion tons detached itself from the Antarctic ice shelf and headed into the Atlantic Ocean. As it began to melt, it broke into a number of smaller pieces that presented a definite potential hazard to shipping lanes.

Internet Disinformation

In the same week in September 1998 that President Bill Clinton's grand jury testimony in the Monica Lewinsky affair went out on national and international TV, the following message was relayed around the Internet as an e-mail chain letter. It was received by hundreds of thousands, if not millions of PCs and business computers.

"Public media should not contain explicit or implied descriptions of sex acts. Our society should be purged of the perverts who provide the media with pornographic material while pretending it has some redeeming social value under the public's right to know."—Kenneth Starr, *60 Minutes* interview with Diane Sawyer, 1987.

Initially, the majority of those who saw it was convinced that the quote was genuine and reacted according to their feelings about Special Prosecutor Starr, the primary agent of the president's humiliation. How many of us can remember what was on *60 Minutes* more than a decade ago anyway? The few diligent individuals who checked were quick to put it out on the net that the thing was a hoax, but that was only after a number of days in circulation. In addition to the revelation that the Kenneth Starr quote was a phony, a second e-mail chain letter—The **Clinton Death List**—appeared, presumably originating from the other political extreme, itemizing all the suspicious deaths that have occurred around Clinton's friends and associates during his rise to power.

A similar Internet e-mail blitz occurred when DJ Howard Stern persuaded his listeners to vote a character known as Hank the Angry Drunken Dwarf to the top of the *People* poll of the hundred most beautiful people of 1998 and beat out Leonardo DiCaprio in the process. The essential difference was that the Hank prank made use of Stern's huge radio audience and their access to e-mail and the net, while the Starr joke was a purely grassroots phenomenon with no centralized motivation. Folks simply read the quote and gleefully forwarded it to all their friends.

Internet Karma

The original function of the Internet was for the military to have an alternative, computer-based means of communication in the event that nuclear attack should knock out the more conventional systems. Now, among other things, the Internet provides easy access to lingerie fashion shows for the masses. Maybe there is hope yet.

Invaders, The

In this 1967-68 one-hour ABC television drama series, architect David Vincent—played by Roy Thinnes—stumbled across evidence of a secret alien invasion of Earth. Because the aliens looked exactly like regular human beings except for slightly deformed pinky fingers, Vincent had a hard time convincing his fellow citizens of the present, but far from clear, danger. *The Invaders* is now cited by alien conspiracy debunkers as one of the cultural origins of **alien abduction** recollections under hypnosis. At the other extreme, some alien conspiracy theorists see it as an attempt at an early warning. At the time of airing, the ABC network publicity department stirred that pot by leaking stories of flying saucers sighted overhead during location filming of the show. *The Invaders* was a Quinn-Martin production.

Is God Punishing Us?

In the wake of the Los Angeles riots and the Northridge earthquake, the local NBC *Channel Four News*, in all seriousness, ran a three-part series titled "Is God Punishing Us?"

J

Jacobson, Max

In the early 1960s, Max Jacobson was known around New York and Washington as Dr. Feelgood, although his medical credentials were frequently in doubt. He was neither a member of the American Medical Association nor affiliated with any conventional hospital. Jacobson's specialty was administering injections of his special solution to celebrities, and he counted Eddie Fisher and Truman Capote among his hundreds of patients. By far his most famous patient was John F. Kennedy, at the time the president of the United States. Although Jacobson made extravagant claims for his "magic shots," they were, in fact, little more than large doses of meth**amphetamine** laced with steroids and animal cells. When the FDA warned the president against Jacobson, JFK's response was the same as many of Jacobson's patients who received similar warnings: "I don't care if it's horse piss. It works."

During the Cuban Missile Crisis of October 1962, Kennedy had Jacobson on twenty-four-hour call, and it is more than likely that while he and Nikita Khrushchev engaged in nuclear brinkmanship, JFK may have been flying on speed. Oddly, because we're still here, it must have worked. In 1975, Jacobson's license to practice medicine was revoked after he was found guilty of fraud and forty-eight counts of unprofessional conduct.

John Wayne

It is probably not a good idea to absolutely trust a man who has the first names "John Wayne..." as in John Wayne Gacey or John Wayne Bobbitt.

Jones, Candy

Candy Jones, a leading New York fashion model in the 1940s and 1950s and the wife of radio personality Long John Nebel, is one of the best documented cases of an unwilling agent of the **CIA** created by a combination of drugs, hypnosis, and intensive mind-control programming. After exhibiting a number of disturbing personality swings, she took an early course of hypnotic regression therapy, during which things that had been done to her by the agency gradually emerged. Seemingly all through the 1950s, the CIA had used her as a deep-cover spy, sending her on primarily courier missions to the Far East under a false name and in a full hypnotic trance. When her mission was complete, she returned to her former life with no memory of what had happened. Her story is chronicled in the book *The Control of Candy Jones* by Donald Bain.

Journalists

When Philip Graham was editor of the *Washington Post* in the 1950s, a **CIA** operative told him, in reference to the availability of journalists, to spread propaganda and disinformation for the agency, "you could get a journalist cheaper than a good call girl."

K

Kachinas

The Native American Hopi traditionally believe that a race called the Kachinas, spirit-like beings from other planets, originally instructed them in agricultural techniques and delivered the philosophical and moral guidelines that shaped Hopi culture.

Kafka, Franz

If the title "Godfather of Modern Paranoia" should be awarded to any one individual, it has to be Franz Kafka, the tubercular Czech novelist whose works, such as *The Trial*, *The Castle*, and *The Penal Colony*, presented horrific visions of an all-powerful tyrant bureaucracy and individuals in nightmarish situations that they can neither escape from nor resolve. The greatest irony is that Kafka's work might have gone unread except that a friend betrayed him. Prior to his death in 1924, Kafka ordered that his work be destroyed. Fortunately for the world of literature, his executor, Max Brod, decided otherwise and had it published.

Kentucky Fried Chicken

Colonel Harlan Sanders's closely guarded secret recipe for the "original" coating mix on Kentucky Fried Chicken was analyzed, and it turned out to be nothing more than skim milk, flour, eggs, salt, black pepper, and plenty o' finger-licking monosodium glutamate. No trace was found of the Colonel's highly advertised "eleven herbs and spices." The only real secret is the KFC patented pressure cooking process. Seems you can't even trust a fat, jolly, old guy in a white suit.

Kilgallen, Dorothy

Although scarcely remembered today, Dorothy Kilgallen was a major media celebrity of the 1950s and early 1960s. She had a popular column in the *New York Journal American* and was a regular panelist on the hit TV game show *What's My Line?* In the fall of 1965, she used her considerable journalistic clout to interview Jack Ruby in his Texas prison cell. According to her confidante and long-time companion, Mrs. Earl T. Smith, Kilgallen returned from the interview elated, convinced that she was going to "break open the Kennedy case." Unfortunately, she never lived to write her story. A few days later, on November 8, 1965, she died in her home at age 52. The cause of death was recorded as "ingestion of alcohol and barbiturates." Mrs. Smith died just two days later of causes that have never been explained. Just two more of the mysterious deaths that seemed to follow the **assassination of John F. Kennedy** like the tail of some sinister comet.

Korzybski, Xandor

Xandor Korzybski is the undisputed bullgoose cybernetic doomsayer. Here is a snatch of his unique prose style—"DEAR HAPLESS BLEATING SACRIFICIAL LAMBS: This may be my last communiqué. We're on collision course with Eschaton. Time and complexity are going asymptotic as we accelerate towards the Singularity. Evil too accelerates: the one world **Illuminati** have recently struck two more heartless, heavy blows intended to test public reaction, serve as a warning to armed survivalists, mind manipulate us all into apocalyptic mega-paranoia, and justify takeover by the secret government."

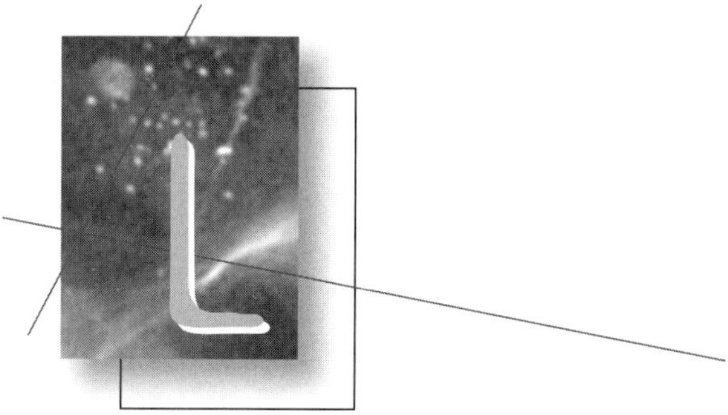

LANDSAT-GIS

One new technology emerging in time for the millennium is the police utilization of geosynchronous LANDSAT satellites linked to Geographical Information Systems. Currently, these systems are used for weather and military surveillance, but as soon as the year 2000, they may be used to watch the movements of tens of thousands of electronically tagged individuals and automobiles in the largest U.S. metropolitan areas. In the future, Big Brother will be watching you from space.

LDE

Long before NASA instigated the Search for Extra Terrestrial Intelligence (SETI), the phenomenon known as Long Delayed Echoes (LDE) convinced a number of scientists experimenting with radio in the 1920s that something might be out there. Radio signals transmitted from Earth would quite regularly come bouncing back, some after just a few seconds while others took a matter of days to return. The effect could not be explained, unless something was picking up the signals in space and retransmitting them. The LDE effect continued to be noted until the mid-1930s, when it appeared to cease. If something had been out there, it had seemingly packed up and gone home.

Leaning Tower of Pisa, The

If it's lucky, the Italian landmark built in 1173 will have another hundred years, and then it will collapse as the walls become unable to hold its weight. The problem has always been that the tower was built on soft sand that could not properly support it. It's been known for some time that the angle, of lean is progressively increasing despite all efforts to strengthen and shore up the famous structure, and when it reaches a certain critical angle, that will be the end of the Tower of Pisa. The tower has been closed to the public since 1990 in an effort to minimize the damage, but the tilt continues to become more acute. Computer expert Lillian Schwartz of Bell Labs has endeavored, by use of a carefully created computer model, to discover what exactly that critical angle might be, and the news is not good for the Pisa tourist industry and lovers of twelfth-century architecture. The Leaning Tower of Pisa is currently leaning at an angle of 5.6 degrees, and another 1.4 degrees will doom it. At 7 degrees, it becomes the Falling Tower of Pisa.

Louie Louie

The bottom line was that no one could make out the lyrics to the song "Louie Louie"—either on the original 1955 recording by Richard Berry and The Pharaohs or on the 1963 hit by The Kingsmen—and that was where all the trouble began. Despite all claims to the contrary and explanations that the song was really about a guy sailing away to sea, teenagers in the early 1960s, almost in a strange form of mass mindset, firmly believed that the lyrics to "Louie Louie" were somehow obscene. Hand-copied transcriptions of the supposed "dirty" lyrics were passed around in high schools, and the conviction that these were the actual recorded lyrics became even more ingrained.

The same idea reached the Federal Communications Commission, and using FBI agents and resources, the FCC began a two-year investigation of the song. It was supposedly the first time that a rock 'n' roll song had been investigated by the federal government. Around the same time, the state of Indiana went one better and banned all airplay of the version by The Kingsmen. The FCC was never able to prove the obscenity of "Louie Louie," but by the time the investigation was concluded, Bob Dylan was in business and rock lyrics would never be understandable again.

Lucas, Henry Lee

It appears that, short of extreme negligence on the part of his guards, Henry Lee Lucas, considered for years the archetypal **serial killer**, will spend the rest of his life in jail without the possibility of parole. In July of 1998, the death sentence imposed on him by a Texas court was commuted by Governor George Bush Jr. For many on both sides of the capital punishment controversy, this seemed something of a strange move on the part of the governor, the Republican son of Republican president George W. Bush. Bush Jr. has always been a major proponent of the death penalty, and since coming to office he has turned down the clemency pleas of condemned criminals who might seem a good deal more deserving than Lucas.

Lucas was an itinerant drifter who was institutionalized as a teenager and later became the subject of a cult classic motion picture, *Henry: Portrait of a Serial Killer.* After his capture he confessed to a total of nearly two hundred thrill-kill homicides of both men and women. Although a number of his confessions were confirmed, many more appeared to be little more than gruesome fantasies, and no trace could be found of some of the supposed victims, even though Lucas led detectives to alleged grave sites. Cynics began to claim that Lucas was using these "confessions" both as a means of self-aggrandizement and as a bizarre source of days away from jail. But others pointed out that Lucas, who was abused as a child—his mother, an alcoholic prostitute, took delight in killing his pets in front of him—could be highly disturbed on a number of levels with a need to confess as strong as the need to kill. It was the argument that Lucas might suffer from a complex and multi-level form of insanity that appeared to sway Governor Bush.

Lustmord

The German language has a word for it, *Lustmord*, quite literally the pleasure or delight taken in the act of murder.

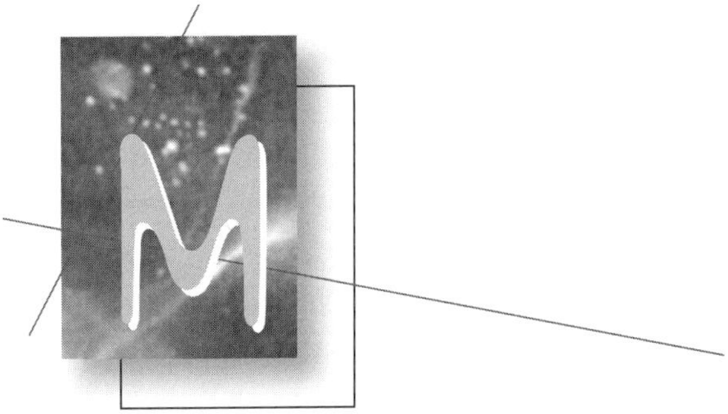

Magnetism

One of the more esoteric revelations during the compiling of this book was realizing just how many conspiracy theories involve magnetism in one form or another. (See: **Cell Phones**, **Deathray, Maser**, **Nazi Flying Saucers**, **PANDORA**, **The Philadelphia Experiment**, **Project HAARP**, **Chan Thomas**, **Dick Tracy**, and **The Tunguska Explosion**.)

Majestic 12

As we bid farewell to the twentieth century, **Majestic 12** (MJ12) has to be the prime contender for the most incredible conspiracy theory of them all, if for no other reason that it provided the basis for the success of **The X-Files**. The story is told in its most developed form by theorists like William Cooper and the infamous Commander X, author of *The Cosmic Patriot Files*. They say that after the crash of one UFO in Aztec, Nevada, and another near White Sands Proving Ground, the primary missile test site of the time, a total of seventeen extraterrestrial bodies were recovered from the wrecks. Then a live alien was discovered wandering in the desert after a slightly later crash near the town of **Roswell**, New Mexico. A security clampdown, more complete than the one imposed on the Manhattan Project and the development of the atom bomb, was organized by a combination of the **CIA** and the Air Force under the direction of an eminent advisory body code-named Majestic 12.

In 1951, the surviving ET fell ill, and with human doctors baffled, it was allowed to phone home. The aliens arrived three years later. Their first landing took place in a remote desert location, and in fact, the film *Close Encounters of the Third Kind* is a thinly fictionalized version of the actual event. After this initial contact, the aliens arrived in force, landed at Muroc (now Edwards) Air Force Base, and met with President Dwight Eisenhower. Recognizing that humanity didn't stand a chance against the highly advanced ETs, Eisenhower essentially negotiated a conditional surrender of humanity whereby the CIA—taking their orders from MJ12 and **The New World Order**—would gradually prepare the Earth for colonization. A few days later, Eisenhower suffered a non-fatal heart attack. All that has happened since has been a direct result of this secret alien infiltration.

The basis of all this theorizing rests with a set of documents known to UFO/conspiracy buffs as the Majestic 12 papers. They are a set of an alleged top-secret government document relating to the establishment of the twelve-man team of distinguished scientists, senior military officers, and respected political figures who had been given the unenviable task of reporting to the president on the problem of these highly advanced visiting aliens. Among the documents is a briefing paper from the MJ12 group that was submitted to Eisenhower during the transition before he assumed the presidency in January of 1953.

The story of how the supposed MJ12 documents were made public is almost as fantastic as the supposed contents. Originally, they came into the possession of TV documentary maker Jaime Shandera. A roll of exposed film was delivered to his home in a plain brown envelope by an unknown source. At the time, Shandera was working on a UFO conspiracy documentary with author William Moore, who had previously published a book on the supposed Roswell flying saucer crash, and Stanton Friedman, a nuclear physicist with an all-consuming interest in the UFO phenomenon. Although Shandera, Moore, and Friedman decided to keep the MJ12 papers under wraps while they attempted to verify their authenticity, the immediate reaction when they went public was one of skepticism and disbelief. Even among the highly paranoid, the MJ12 papers were simply too good to be true. If real, they proved conclusively that the U.S. government was involved in a massive conspiracy with sinister beings from other worlds.

One of the first strikes against them being the genuine article was the presence of William Moore. Not only had he written a book about Roswell, but the MJ12 papers amply confirmed everything he put in the book. Worse than that, he had been publicly accused by rival UFO conspiracy theorists of being a government plant, spreading disinformation, and even playing a role in the widely-publicized drama surrounding the mental collapse of UFO researcher **Paul Bennewitz**. Many believed Bennewitz had been deliberately driven to a breakdown by government agents. Another sticking point was what purported to be a list of the members of the MJ12 group. Although it included Admiral Roscoe Hillenkoetter, the first Director of the CIA, and James Forrestal, the Secretary of Defense in the Truman Administration, every man on the list was dead by the time the documents became public in 1986.

Since that time the MJ12 debate has swung backward and forward, gathering almost as many conflicting scenarios as the **Kennedy assassination**. The documents are a fraud, period. The documents are a fraud, but their contents are accurate. They're a fraud deliberately perpetrated by a government wanting to conceal an even worse situation. The documents are real and we are all in a great deal of trouble. The story is, of course, fantastic. The problem with immediately dismissing it as laughable, however, is that it's set in a world where the fantastic has been proved, over and over again, to be no laughing matter.

Mansfield, Jayne

Even after more than thirty years, stories still linger that the 1967 death of movie sex-bomb Jayne Mansfield was the result of a Satanic curse that misfired. Mansfield had first showed up at the Church of Satan in San Francisco, run by the notorious Anton LaVey, author of *The Satanic Bible*, wanting LaVey to put a curse on her second husband, Matt Climber, with whom she was engaged in a child-custody suit. After a win in the courts, Mansfield was sufficiently convinced of LaVey's power to become an ardent Satan worshiper and LaVey follower. He even had photographs of Mansfield on her knees before a robed and horned Anton LaVey, engaged in celebrating a black mass. Later, when her young son, Zoltan, was mauled by a lion at the Jungleland Wild Animal Park, she credited LaVey's intervention with saving the boy's life.

Unfortunately, this relationship with LaVey caused problems with Jayne's then current boyfriend, Sam Brody, who began threatening LaVey. LaVey hit back by supposedly cursing Brody and called Mansfield a number of times, telling her to stay away from Brody and especially not to drive with him. Jayne ignored LaVey and on June 29, 1967, she and Brody were both killed when the car in which they were traveling hit a truck on a highway outside New Orleans. When LaVey heard that Jayne had been decapitated in the crash, he reportedly blamed himself, having accidentally cut the head off a picture of her while the curse on Brody was in effect.

LaVey may have blamed himself, but it didn't stop him cashing in on the attendant publicity. *The Satanic Bible* became an occult best-seller, topping a half million sales. LaVey became the big-ticket American media Satanist and other celebrities, including Sammy Davis Jr., flocked to his church.

Manson, Marilyn

According to his own statement on the October 5, 1998, *Howard Stern Show* on the E! entertainment cable-TV channel, Marilyn Manson, the controversial rock idol, is the child of a Vietnam combat veteran and Agent Orange victim. In the days following the 1999 **high school slaughter** in Littleton, Colorado, his name was bandied about in the press and on TV as one of the major influences on the killers, Eric Harris and Dylan Klebold, even though by their own Web site statements, they were actually into more obscure, quasi-Germanic, goth/death metal bands like KMFDM and Rammstein.

Marijuana

From a practical, commonsense point of view, the reasons for marijuana remaining illegal under all circumstances seem to grow more controversial as more studies are done on the medical effects of the drug. Aside from its now clearly demonstrated efficacy in the treatment of glaucoma and mitigating the side effects of AZT and cancer therapies, a recent Japanese study discovered that THC, the active ingredient in marijuana, actually protected the brain cells of rats from the damage that can be caused by oxygen deprivation.

Marilyn Monroe's Diary

Although many friends and acquaintances—including Shelley Winters—recount how Marilyn Monroe was a compulsive diarist, her diary vanished within hours of her death. According to Robert Slatzer, another long-time friend, "For years, Marilyn kept scribbled notes of conversations to help her remember things." After Marilyn's supposed suicide on August 5, 1962, the diary went to the office of Los Angeles Coroner's Aide Lionel Grandison, but by the next day it had disappeared, and according to Grandison, "someone had removed it from the list of items that had been brought in for investigation." The disappearance of the diary might not be so significant if it wasn't for all the other missing evidence pertaining to the death of the movie goddess. In a matter of days after her death, her phone records were gone, apparently impounded by the Secret Service, and by 1966 the entire file on her death was missing, including the original death report. When, in that year, Los Angeles Mayor Sam Yorty requested the file from the LAPD, he was told that "it isn't here."

In 1985, an anonymous former FBI agent claimed, "The FBI did remove certain Monroe records. I was on a visit to California when Monroe died, and became aware of the removal of records from my Los Angeles colleagues. I knew there had been some people there, Bureau personnel who normally wouldn't have been there—agents from out of town. They were there on the scene immediately, as soon as she died, before anyone realized what happened. It had to be on the instructions of someone high up, higher even than **Hoover**...either the attorney general or the president."

Were Jack and Bobby Kennedy, both of whom reputedly had affairs with Marilyn, using the FBI to protect their reputations? We'll probably never know. It would seem, though, if those in power don't want we the people seeing conspiracies behind every bush and on every grassy knoll, they could be a little more deft with their cover-ups.

MASER

Microwave Amplification by Stimulated Radiation is a device that generates highly stable electro**magnetic** waves by use of the natural oscillations of an atom or molecule. Masers are low-power microwave (LMP) weapons that, when targeting a human brain, are capable of creating auditory hallucinations akin to the kind of voices-in-the-head reportedly experienced by paranoid schizophrenics, or in the bicameral minds of our ancient forbears. Claims are made that masers have supposedly been issued to many federal agencies, including the FBI, **NSA**, NRO, **CIA**, Army Intelligence, Naval Intelligence, Department of Energy, Defense Investigative Services, DIA, **DEA**, Justice Department, Department of Treasury, and BATF. But the maser is surrounded by an almost total media blackout, and no record exists of one ever having been employed in field conditions or on active service. Rumors did circulate that masers and similar weapons may have been deployed, but not used, during the siege of the **Branch Davidian** compound outside of Waco.

Thus, the next time you see someone talking to an invisible companion, just wonder. Are they crazy, or maybe they were just zapped by a maser in the hands of **The New World Order** or whomever? Apparently, shielding is not possible against maser emissions.

Mayan Calendar

The Mayan Calendar, one of the most accurate calendars ever created by a so-called "primitive people," appears to show that time itself will run out in the year 2012. No floods, earthquakes, crashing comets, or other apocalyptic events. Not even a fat lady singing. Merely the end of everything and total nothingness.

Mean Old Witches

When asked years later about what had become of the dozens of young hippie women on the fringes of the Manson Family who maintained their nonstop vigil outside the Los Angeles Hall of Justice during the 1970–71 Tate/La Bianca murder trial, Charlie Manson merely smiled. "They're still around, except now they're mean old witches."

Meier, Eduard (Billy)

If commercial success and near-cult leader status can be considered a mark of success in the UFO community, then Eduard (Billy) Meier is possibly the most successful UFO contactee of the twentieth century. Billy Meier first surfaced in 1975 when he claimed to be in contact with an advanced alien race from the constellation of the Pleiades (also known to astronomers as the "Seven Sisters"). Meier's story was that the aliens had paid him over a hundred visits at his idyllic Alpine farm, and that he was the sole Earthly recipient of Pleiadian wisdom. Not only that, but he also had over 12,000 extraordinarily clear, daylight photographs of the Pleiadian "beamships," plus 8mm movie footage to prove it. The Pleiadian wisdom, a very simplistic peace and love, protect the planet message, seemed to strike a chord with New Agers and ex-hippies, and almost overnight, Meier had become a one-man Pleiadian industry turning out books, posters, and videocassettes.

Considerable doubt has been cast on the authenticity of Meier's photographs and films—indeed, even to the untrained eye they appear to be badly-designed or constructed models, some involving Christmas tree ornaments, dangled from concealed thread, or posed in a way to confuse perspective. But this doesn't seem to deter the large numbers of true believers. Even when it was revealed that photos purporting to be of a Pleiadian called "Asket" were taken at a Swedish modeling agency, the faithful continued to accept Meier without question. They also didn't seem to be daunted by the fact that the idea of a race from a planet in the Pleiades "system" was an astronomical absurdity. The Pleiades are not a star system but merely a constellation. The seven stars that comprise it are, in fact, nowhere near each other in interstellar space, they only look like that when observed from the Earth.

Today, Billy Meier is reputed to live in seclusion and multi-partner polygamy in a cult-like commune, supported by donations from his followers/acolytes.

Militia Movement

What has become known as the Militia Movement scared the hell out of Americans in the weeks after the 1995 bombing of the Federal Building in Oklahoma City. Both the media and the FBI seemed so totally unprepared for it that for the first twenty-four hours after the horror, the hunt was on for Arab terrorists. It was only when the trail that would eventually lead to Timothy McVeigh was picked up that anyone started to think in terms of a homegrown, white male, blue-collar conspiracy. That no one but a few fringe observers had any clue that militias were coming was not only surprising but also unforgivable. The evolution of the Militia Movement was a predictably classic case of a number of parallel but previously unrelated groups coming together to create a terrible momentum of hate and anger. It should have been studied as a case history in the making rather than ignored or completely overlooked by news media that pretend to have their ears to the ground and a government that spends millions on supposed national security.

The three main political building blocks that were cemented together to form the foundations of the Militia Movement included the old-style American Nazis—groups like the Aryan Brotherhood, the White Aryan Resistance, and even the Ku Klux Klan. There were the survivalists of the 1970s and early 1980s, who had waited in armed and often lonely readiness for an apocalyptic breakdown of society that never came, and the hard-line gun lobbyists, who were becoming increasingly alarmed after even George Bush had given half-hearted support to a ban on assault weapons. Once these were in place, it became possible to attract other increasingly alienated but previously unorganized individuals—the tax resisters for whom Ross Perot was too tame, farm communities who felt they'd been betrayed by both big business and big government, assorted skinheads, crazies and *Soldier of Fortune* fantasists, and the anti-Federalist Posse Comitatus types who skirmished with federal agents in the rural Midwest in the early 1980s. Probably most important of all were angry white males who believed, maybe wrongly but nonetheless fervently, that they had been deprived of both political power and a voice in the era of affirmative action and political correctness.

A certain amount of ideological compromise obviously had to go down before this kind of coalition could coalesce. The neo-Nazis had to tone down some of their more overt racism, the survivalists had to come in from the cold and begin to actively interrelate, and gun owners needed to accept a level of organizational involvement they had not previously exhibited. This appears to have been achieved by uniting against a common target and a common set of symbolic bad guys. These came in the form of the highly paranoid scenario of **The New World Order** taking over the U.S., suspending the Constitution and imposing World Government by force—complete with its almost science fiction trappings of foreign troops, **FEMA** involvement, and **black helicopters**.

Even though it was heavily promoted by conservative talk radio, in the radical right press, and on the Internet, this was still a tenuous thread on which to hang a potential right-wing revolution. The Militia Movement would probably never have gained the impetus it did had not the Feds, under both Bush and Clinton, seemed determined to give it all the confirmation it needed. First, the fatal FBI mishandling of the standoff with Randy Weaver and his family at Ruby Ridge, then the disastrous first AFT raid on the **Branch Davidian** compound at Waco, and finally the FBI going in with tanks and helicopters to end the Waco siege in an authoritarian orgy of fire and death, live on TV, appeared to say it all. Images of federal agents with automatic weapons, neo-ninja body armor, and kevlar helmets, as well as the certain knowledge that in flames and black smoke at Waco, small children were being burned to death in what was, after all, a church, proved so shocking it was almost inevitable someone like Timothy McVeigh got the idea that something drastic and spectacular must be done.

Since the Oklahoma bombing and the McVeigh trial, the Militia Movement has hardly been courting publicity and has largely dropped out of the media spotlight. On the other hand, it still has its weapons, its camouflage gear, and is still out in the woods on weekends. It's hardly a mindset that packs up and goes home. The movement could fragment as the original coalition comes unglued, or it could evolve further into something even more hidden and dangerous.

MKULTRA

MKULTRA, the in-house research group formed after Allen Dulles took over the directorship of the **CIA** in 1953, had the basic brief to explore the possibilities and techniques for controlling the human mind. It's no exaggeration to say that MKULTRA and all the similar units that followed in its increasingly bizarre footsteps were probably more responsible for the public's fear of the agency than any other factor. If the CIA is able to mess with our very minds, what hope can there be for the free citizen remaining that way? With MKULTRA, the CIA boldly went where no intelligence agency had gone before. The only possible exception was Hitler's Gestapo. During the course of its ten-year, highly secret life, MKULTRA is on record as having tested large quantities of LSD and other mind altering drugs on human subjects—either student volunteers or convicted federal criminals. The unit is documented as having developed advanced brainwashing techniques, including hypnotism and sensory deprivation, and implanting electronic control devices in the skulls of animals and quite possibly humans.

Allen Dulles's original rationale for setting up an operation with a name that sounded like low-budget science fiction was a reaction to the Communist show trials in the decade after World War II. There, defendants publicly confessed to all manner of treason and crimes against the state that they clearly would not have ever been in a position to commit. The fear was that the Soviets might be developing a range of mind-bending truth drugs and other direct psychological control techniques. After studying available films and audiotapes of the trials, the agency issued a Special Security Memorandum declaring that "some unknown force had been used." If the Reds had mind control, then obviously the U.S. couldn't afford to be without the same capability. The aims of MKULTRA didn't stop at the development of simple, more efficient brainwashing and interrogation through possible "truth drugs." Other goals appear to include the creation of "robot" mind-controlled spies and assassins, and the use of psychedelic drugs as weapons of mass psyops warfare. One MKULTRA researcher admitted, "we thought about the possibility of putting LSD in a city water supply and having the citizens wander around in a more or less happy state, not terribly interested in defending themselves."

It's also possible that in the guise of investigating the viability of a "**psycho-civilized society**," the scientists and agents who ran MKULTRA may have contemplated using drugs on a mass scale to create a "brave new world" totally controlled by the agency. The Orwellian nightmare of a docile civilian population driven like sheep, obeying the orders of their self-appointed Agency masters without hesitation or question, was seemingly too tempting a vision to ignore. If this seems far-fetched, evidence has been presented by individuals like John Marks in his book, *The Search for the "Manchurian Candidate,"* that MKULTRA and the CIA experimented regularly on unsuspecting sections of the civilian population. In the early

1960s, an aerosol-style drug delivery system was tested in the New York subway system. In this instance, only an inert chemical was used instead of a psycho-active drug. Certain residents of San Francisco had been less lucky in the mid- to late 1950s when a one-time federal narcotics agent, George White, doing contract work for the CIA, set up a string of clandestine "safe houses." In them, CIA-hired prostitutes would slip the drug to their unsuspecting clients while the boys from MKULTRA watched and filmed the results from behind false walls and one-way mirrors. White may also have later been instrumental in making LSD available as a popular street drug and inadvertently responsible for the 1967 "Summer of Love."

Headed by Ph.D. chemist Dr. Sidney Gottlieb, and protected from government interference and oversight by future CIA Director Richard Helms, MKULTRA inhabited a looking-glass world where black could easily be white, and nothing was what it seemed. For ten years it went its own way with virtually unlimited funds and minimal accountability. When, in 1963, President John Kennedy attempted to stage a major reorganization of the CIA after the disastrously aborted invasion of Cuba at the Bay of Pigs, some of MKULTRA's more outrageous programs began to come to light. The project was closed down, but not before Helms and Gottlieb organized the shredding of most of the unit's records so that the full scope of its experiments—or the damage they caused—would never be known.

With the closure of MKULTRA, the intention was for the U.S. government to get out of the mind-control business altogether. Unfortunately, as was revealed by the 1975 Rockefeller Commission and other subsequent probes under the Freedom of Information Act, MKULTRA disappeared in name only. Mind-control research has continued practically uninterrupted through to the present day under new code names like MKSEARCH, MKNAOMI, ARTICHOKE, OFTEN, GRILL FLAME, and **PANDORA**.

Mole People

One urban legend that it is growing and multiplying upon itself is that of the Mole People, who supposedly live in the sewers, storm drains, water conduit tunnels, subways, and even abandoned civil defense fallout shelters beneath the major cities of the U.S. They are not only growing in number but also mutating into creatures/beings that are something other than human. (In some respects, they parallel the Russian account of the **Moscow Dog Boy**.) The nugget of established fact behind these stories is the well-documented community of the homeless who live in the multi-level tunnels under Manhattan's Grand Central Station. Many of these people are seriously deranged and generally left alone by New York City transit cops because they're too much trouble to root out, and once rooted, become the city's responsibility. As long ago as the 1960s, stories circulated about a gang of near feral and stone-deaf children and teenagers who called themselves the Crazy Homicides. They lived in the subways and were extremely dangerous—indeed, to the point of being homicidal—when confronted, and may have been the model for the fictional teen gang of deaf mutes known as the Ducky Boys in Richard Price's novel *The Wanderers* and the movie that followed.

These tales of the Mole People may have evolved from those of the Crazy Homicides, cross-fertilized by the time-honored myth of albino alligators in the sewers but now applied to human beings. With the Mole People, however, the envelope of fantasy is pushed to the extreme. The Mole People are credited with early development of such attributes as feline-style night vision and webbed feet. They also have organized an extensive and functioning Satanic religion of the underground and believe themselves to be living in Hell (which hardly seems so unreasonable). It's possible that pop culture may have had an influence on the concept of the Mole People in the form of the movies *C.H.U.D.* and *C.H.U.D II* (C.H.U.D.= Cannibalistic Humanoid Underground Dwellers)—in which evil sewer derelicts come up to street level in the dead of night and snack on human flesh—and maybe even the 1951 *Superman and the Mole Men*.

It's one theory regarding the genesis of an urban legend.

Moon Landing

An estimated 600 million people watched the moon landings, but since that time, claims have never subsided that the entire thing was a fake—a piece of elaborate government science fiction shot in a secret studio in the California desert. In 1974, ex-Northrop engineer Bill Kaysing published his book *We Never Went to the Moon* making exactly that claim, and the story has surfaced at regular intervals ever since. The latest individual to doubt the authenticity of the moon landings is English photographer David Perly who, in a 1997 edition of the British magazine *Fortean Times*, pointed out computer-enhanced lighting anomalies in the photographs supposedly taken on the moon by the various Apollo missions. According to Perly, these provided proof that they must have been shot on Earth with planned studio lighting. NASA optical engineers quickly countered that Perly had neglected to factor in the light from the Earth and the highly reflective, grey-white surface of the moon.

Morgan, Vicki

Since her murder in 1983, model and party girl Vicki Morgan has provided a minor but seductive sidebar to the conspiracy theories of the **Reagan** era. Morgan had been the long-time mistress of Alfred Bloomingdale, the founder of the Diner's Club and heir to the Bloomingdale's department store fortune. Bloomingdale was also a close friend of Ronald Reagan and a member of his "kitchen cabinet." On July 7, 1983, Morgan was found beaten to death in her Hollywood apartment. Her roommate, Marvin Pancost, immediately confessed to the slaying.

Until the backstory started to unfold, it seemed to be nothing more than another murky murder in the Hollywood shadows. Doubts began with the story that a year earlier, when Bloomingdale had been hospitalized for throat cancer, his wife, Betsy, attempted to take Vicki out of her husband's sexual loop by cutting off the money. An angry Vicki hit back with the threat to go public, claiming she had acted as hostess at regular S&M, whip and bondage parties thrown by Bloomingdale for prominent figures in the Reagan administration, and she had videotapes to prove it. Five days after the murder, attorney Robert Steinberg claimed he had the Bloomingdale orgy tapes but was unable to produce them when ordered by a court. They had been mysteriously stolen from his briefcase.

Pancost went to jail for life and the Vicki Morgan story should have ended there except that weird tidbits of information continued to surface. Pancost turned out to have a history of confessing to crimes he did not commit, all the way back to when he tried to take the blame for the Tate/La Bianca murders. The LAPD investigation was revealed to be badly botched and the crime scene had not been sealed for twenty-four hours. These details were more than enough to start the conspiracy mill grinding. The popular theory was that someone in the Reagan camp used Bloomingdale's intelligence connections—he was a Reagan appointee to the Foreign Intelligence Advisory Board—to silence Morgan before copies of the sex party tapes could bring down the Republican presidency.

Morrison, Jim

In common with James Dean, Marilyn Monroe, and **Elvis Presley**, myths and rumors have surrounded the memory of controversial 1960s rock star Jim Morrison since his death in Paris in 1971. As with the majority of dead legends, the most common stories are those of his not being dead at all but living in seclusion, away from the stress of stardom—in rural Mexico, in a small town on the edge of the Sahara, in an Indian ashram, or in the remote jungles of the Amazon. These largely seem to be a symptom of fan denial, and the more time that passes without the legend revealing himself and returning to public life, the less credence can be given. The second wave of stories usually concerns some real or imagined mystery, conspiracy, or cover-up surrounding the celebrity's death. Was Marilyn murdered, did Elvis overdose, or did Courtney kill Kurt? In Morrison's case, rumors in the French capital at the time of his death have lingered, claiming that far from dying of a heart attack in the bathroom of his apartment, he in fact overdosed on heroin in a Left Bank nightclub. Friends and hangers-on managed to get his body home in a cab and placed Jim naked in a tub of warm water, to confuse the time of death, before calling the police.

One of the most recent and certainly one of the stranger rumors spread about Jim Morrison, initially by word of mouth but later on the Internet, was that Morrison was a Frankenstein creation of the U.S. government. This odd rock 'n' roll fable claims that Morrison was designed by either the FBI's COINTELPRO operation that spied on 1960s radicals and attempted to infiltrate the anti-Vietnam war movement, or the **CIA**'s Chaos Program that employed much the same aims and methods, perhaps with a little chemical or hypnotic help from the mind-control experts at **MKULTRA**. The idea was seemingly that Morrison, a revolutionary rock 'n' roll loose cannon in the best of times, would trigger some spectacular incident that would give the authorities the excuse to crack down in a major way on rock 'n' rollers with radical or anti-war ties.

Most of Morrison's surviving friends and associates and even members of his band, The Doors, dismiss this as nothing more than the heated imaginings of creative paranoids. Jim Morrison was quite a rock 'n' roll rebel, crazy enough on his own without any programming by the government. Perhaps the saddest postscript to the entire Jim Morrison story is that despite his continuing role as a twentieth-century rock 'n' roll icon and the ongoing interest in his life, death, work, and excesses, no one has taken particularly good care of Jim since his death. Certainly no one, to paraphrase the old blues song, has seen that his grave was kept clean.

Although he was buried in Pere Lachaise cemetery in Paris, beside such luminaries as Molière, Balzac, Oscar Wilde, Sarah Bernhardt, and Marcel Proust, it took years for the most meager of monuments to be erected on his grave, despite the fact that his record company and his old comrades in The Doors were making millions from his memory and the constant recycling of his recordings. In addition, the fans who constantly visited the Paris gravesite were a disgustingly messy and irreverent bunch of jerks. The casually abandoned garbage and the graffiti they scrawled and spray painted on the surrounding and truly magnificent tombs of other artists made the Morrison gravesite a blot on the entire historic graveyard. By 1998, the lack of upkeep on Jim's grave brought the Pere Lachaise authorities to the point of demanding that Morrison's body be exhumed and buried elsewhere. Proving that, even in death, one is not safe from eviction by the landlord.

Moscow Dog Boy

In the summer of 1998, according to the British magazine *The Week*, a feral, six-year-old boy called Ivan Mishukov was discovered to have been living with stray dogs for two years in the cellars of derelict buildings after being abandoned by his parents in 1996. Little Ivan apparently survived the bitter winters in the Russian capital by retreating with his canine companions into the Moscow sewer system, where they all slept near underground hot water pipes. He would also beg for food that he then distributed among the dogs. The bonds had become so great that it took police almost a month to separate him from the dogs. Ivan is now in an orphanage but complains that he was "better off with the dogs. They loved and protected me."

Mount Weather

The ultra-secret facility known as Mount Weather, near the small town of Bluemont, Virginia, according to most conspiracy buffs and observers of the intelligence community, was built at massive public cost in the early 1950s as part of a nuclear preparedness civil-defense program called "The Continuity of Government Program." Designed to act as an alternative seat of government in the event of an atomic attack, Mount Weather is reputed to be an underground city complete with offices, dormitories, cafeterias, hospitals, a lake fed with fresh water from underground springs, and even a mass-transit system. It is supposedly fully staffed at all times and able to take over the complete functioning of the government of the United States on extremely short notice. Mount Weather has seemingly been placed on full alert on a number of occasions since it was completed. The first time was during the 1961 Cuban missile crisis, and then subsequently after the **assassination of JFK** in 1963, during the urban riots in 1967 and 1968, and in August 1974 during the post-Watergate Nixon impeachment and resignation crisis.

Mount Weather is also alleged to be the repository for all data gathered on U.S. citizens by the **CIA**, FBI, and other agencies. In 1975, John Tunney, chairman of the Subcommittee on Constitutional Rights, charged that over 100,000 detailed and highly illegal dossiers on U.S. citizens were stored on the Mount Weather computers, and a list of some 15,000 names was maintained of individuals who would be immediately detained in a situation of national emergency. When Tunney's committee questioned General Leslie Bray, director of the Federal Preparedness Agency, about Mount Weather, its function, and its use by the **NSA**, FBI, and CIA, they ran into a stone wall. Bray's reply was brief and uncooperative: "I am not at liberty to describe precisely what is the role and the mission and the capability we have at Mount Weather." As far as anyone knows, it is still there and still in operation. Information is still being gathered, and none of its dossiers have ever been deleted.

Mutant Frogs

In the summer of 1998, Interior Secretary Bruce Babbitt finally addressed a problem that for a number of years has been bothering ecologists, naturalists, and small children who live in the country. Why is it that frogs and other amphibians like newts and toads are dying in large numbers or growing extra legs and other unpleasant deformities? The Taskforce on Amphibian Death and Deformities (TADD) is now in business to get to the bottom of the problem. And if you think this is yet another federal boondoggle, think again. Because frogs spend time both on land and in water, and their highly permeable skin easily absorbs chemicals and pathogens, they are among the first species to react to a seriously poisoned environment. What happens to the frog today is more than likely to happen to humans a few years down the pike. The highest incidence of frog mutation and death seems to occur in Minnesota, across the entire continent of Australia, and on Costa Rican islands, and the reasons for this will be a priority with TADD researchers. They will also be paying particular attention to chemicals known as retenoids, heavy metals, and the effects of ultraviolet light.

N

National Security Agency

Most conspiracy theorists treat the **CIA** as if it were the heart of darkness in the intelligence community, but the National Security Agency is emerging as perhaps occupying an even darker place. The NSA is possibly the most secretive of all the government intelligence agencies—or to be more precise, the most secretive of all the government intelligence agencies that the public knows about. It wasn't until the end of the **Reagan** administration and the Iran-Contra scandal that the federal government even officially admitted that it existed. The formal function of the NSA is apparently to oversee all forms of communication and transmission of information. Although it may sound like a fairly narrow brief, it includes everything from computers and encryption to radar and satellite linkage, which in practice, can be made to cover just about anything.

Lawsuits under the Freedom of Information Act in the last decade or so have revealed that the NSA has had its fingers in such varied pies as e-mail interception and UFO research. Perhaps the greatest indication of how the Fort Meade–based agency keeps itself to itself is that even rumors and speculation about it are fairly thin on the ground. While just about everyone who goes to movies, watches TV, or reads Tom Clancy novels knows a good deal about the inner workings of the CIA, the NSA remains a tightly closed book. Even in fiction, it tends only to surface as little more than the shadow super-agency. One theory is that this may well be a deliberate move. While, in comparison, the CIA showboats with its plots and covert ops, it also serves to reassure the public that whether they like it or not, America is holding its own in the James Bond business. This leaves the NSA free to get on with the truly covert under a total screen of metaphoric night and fog.

This relationship appears to be maintained even in the relative innocence of cyberspace. The CIA hosts a fairly user-friendly public Web site with recruiting information and even an area for kids. Visit the NSA homepage, on the other hand, and one is confronted by a vertical button bar with links to such topics as "What Is the NSA?" and "Policy Statement." Hit any of these buttons, however, and *absolutely nothing happens*.

Nazi Flying Saucers

When flying saucers became the hot aerial phenomenon of the late 1940s and early 1950s, one of the first theories—maybe even before the idea was mooted that they were extraterrestrial space vehicles—was that they were some kind of Nazi super-weapon left over from the final days of World War II. The concept of alien spaceships seemed to grab the big numbers in Hollywood and the public imagination. But visions of Adolf Hitler, selected henchmen, and Eva Braun escaping to Argentina in a hovering UFO to be greeted by a delighted Evita Peron did have their adherents. (Although they didn't quite compete with the fantasy of ravening Martians with transparent bubble helmets and exposed brains storming out of disc-shaped craft to carry off Earth's women in their tentacles.)

In his book *Virtual Government,* author Alex Constantine—although he doesn't quite make the claim Hitler escaped by saucer in 1945 from his bunker in the ruins of Berlin—states that all of the objects folks have seen in the sky over the last sixty years have their origins in secret Nazi technology. He says that the Third Reich had electro**magnetic**-powered, disc-shaped aircraft in the air and operational by the end of the war, although it was too late to reverse the German defeat. In support of his claim, he cites the *New York Herald Tribune* of January 2, 1945. "Now, it seems, the Nazis have thrown something new into the night skies over Germany. It is the weird, mysterious **Foo Fighters**, balls that race alongside the wings of Beaufighters flying intruder missions over Germany."

Seemingly, the Foo Fighters were the brainchild of General Hans Kammler, a protege of Heinrich Himmler and the designer of the death machine constructed at Auschwitz. In the effort to create an electromagnetic war plane, the prototype was the Foo Fighter, an unmanned disc guided by a remote television-control system, created by Telefunken and Blaupunkt and intended to stop allied bombers by knocking out their ignition with a powerful electrostatic surge. A whole range of manned electromagnetic craft was in the development stage when the Third Reich collapsed.

The technology fell mainly into the hands of the U.S., which has been working on it ever since, and indeed, that is what is really being hidden at **Area 51**. Constantine goes on to make the case that the entire ET/UFO folklore phenomenon has merely been a cover for the ongoing government research into this revolutionary technology.

Neutron Stars

As if we didn't have enough to worry about already, Aron Dar, a space physicist at the Israel Institute of Technology, believes that we are more than 100,000 years overdue for a lethal blast of cosmic radiation that would wipe out up to 95 percent of animal and plant life on the Earth. What bothers the eminent Israeli scientist is the possibility of our planet being in the wrong place at the wrong time. The wrong time, in this instance, is during the collapse of a pair of neutron stars, a phenomenon in deep space that ultimately creates a black hole. When such an occurrence happens, massive amounts of energy are released, some of it in the form of a tightly focused beam of cosmic rays that can travel up to a million light years before losing their power. God help any inhabited planets that come into range of the spotlight of cosmic rays.

When cosmic rays strike the Earth's atmosphere, they produce high-energy, subatomic particles called *muons* that are highly destructive to all forms of living tissue and can easily penetrate water. They not only pose a threat to all land creatures but also to aquatic life. Under normal circumstances, the ionosphere protects us from most cosmic radiation, but in proximity to a pair of collapsing neutron stars, these natural defenses would be overwhelmed.

Dar calculates that the Earth is affected by an event of this nature approximately every hundred million years—although he goes to some lengths to make it clear he's not claiming it was a neutron star collapse that killed the dinosaurs. Up until the last catastrophe, which seems to have mainly spared insects, the hundred-million-year cycle seemed to be holding up. It has now been twice that time, over 200 million years, since the last near-extinction, and Dar reasons that we are now well overdue for another onslaught of cosmic radiation. If it's any consolation, Dar expects us to get a few days warning for the impending wipeout. The first signs will be a pale blue glow in the sky that will gradually intensify over about eighty-four hours. Not that there's anything we can do to avoid the inevitable, short of a speedy mass evacuation of the planet.

New World Order, The

An essential part of most paranoid belief patterns is a single point of focus—an individual, group, or organization that can be the "one behind it all"—to whom all blame and responsibility can be attached. Some students of mass paranoia, particularly those who define paranoia as the need to impose some manner of quasi-organized structure on what is seen as an impossibly chaotic and hostile world, call this kind of blame placement "the Octopus Syndrome," the idea that all that ails us uncoils like tentacles from a single head.

The George Bush speechwriter who originally coined the phrase "new world order" at the end of the Gulf War made a fundamental but understandable error. Obviously, the intention was to create a ringing—perhaps Churchillian—phrase that summed up the way things would be after the fall of communism and the elimination of minor nuisances like Saddam Hussein. It needed to encapsulate the wonder of a world in which capitalism was the only ideology, and the U.S. was the single benign superpower, bestowing peace and plenty with no evil empire to foul things up. The speechwriter can't be totally blamed, however. The phrase managed to get through the considerable filtration process to which any presidential utterance is now subjected with no one noticing that it had a certain unfortunate echo of Adolf Hitler's New Order for Europe, in which Germany would be the only superpower and Nazism the only ideology.

The Bush advisors may have missed the resonance, but the extreme right militants caught it with a vengeance. It may seem a little strange that our domestic fascists should take exception to a Republican president turning a Hitlerian phrase, but the extreme right—particularly the blue-collar right—never exactly trusted George Bush. They remembered the 1980 Republican primaries when Bush challenged their hero **Ronald Reagan**—claiming to be the voice of moderation and coining the phrase "voodoo economics." They also remembered when Bush was the Ivy League head of the **CIA**, with ties to repugnant internationalist-vested interests like big oil, big banking, the **Bilderburg Group**, the **Tri-lateral Commission** and the Club of Rome. Almost overnight, The New World Order was turned around, and instead of being the force behind the "thousand points of light," it became the lurking darkness behind all that was bad—the head of the armed right's particular octopus.

The hard thing to pin down is exactly who or what The New World Order is—and that's one of its major advantages. While the New World Order remains vague and threatening, anything goes, and at the same time, it avoids the overt racism of the out-and-out neo-Nazis. Most of the usual suspects are tied to the New World Order—the UN, the Vatican, the Rothchilds, the Rockefellers, the Yale Skull and Bones Club, the manufacturers of Prozac, corporate Japan, and even the English monarchy. It doesn't stop there, however. Up the ante and you find the New World Order embracing more arcane anxieties like the **Freemasons**, the Knights Templar, the **Bavarian Illuminati**, and the **Thule Society**. Raise the volume and extreme conspiracist voices like those of ex-Naval Intelligence operative William Cooper and Commander X, author of the impenetrably lunatic Cosmic Patriot Files, can be heard claiming that everything is being run by a cabal of sinister extraterrestrials from the system **Zeta Reticuli** and **Majestic 12**, their traitorous human collaborators.

Whoever or whatever the New World Order may be, all the believers seem to agree on its immediate scenario. The NWO waits—quietly slipping drugs and money to whatever section of the population will use them to create the most chaos—until things are *really bad* in the United States. At that point, their puppet president will declare a state of emergency, suspend the Constitution, and invite in UN troops to restore order. With patriotic Americans rendered helpless by gun control, it will only be a short step to totalitarian slavery.

NORAD

According to information obtained by English UFO researcher Timothy Good, NORAD—North American Aerospace Defense Command, the great western radar shield during the Mutually Assured Destruction superpower nuclear standoff between the U.S. and the Soviets—now has two classifications for unidentified flying objects. Where once they were all classed as UFOs, they are now divided into UFOs and ASPs—Alternative Space Craft. The implication is that some flying saucers are no longer unidentified because NORAD knows exactly what they are.

Nuclear Near Miss

One may have thought that after the breakup of the Soviet Union, the half-century-long fear of an accidental triggering of a nuclear war between

Russia and the U.S. was a thing of the past. Unfortunately, this is far from the case. According to a documentary shown on Britain's Channel 4 TV network in July of 1998, World War III was all but set off in 1995 by the launching of a Norwegian weather research rocket. Russian radar defenses mistook the civilian rocket for a sneak attack by American Trident missiles, and a ten-minute countdown started. After four minutes, missiles carrying trains and submarines were alerted. One minute later, President Boris Yeltsin would have had to decide to issue the code for a retaliatory nuclear strike. Luckily, at this point, it was realized that the rocket's trajectory was taking it in the direction of the Arctic and not into Russia and a stand-down was ordered.

O

Operation Wandering Soul

Operation Wandering Soul was possibly the most bizarre of the psychological warfare operations (psyops) conducted by the **CIA.** It was set in motion during the Vietnam War under auspices of the notorious **Phoenix Program**. Light aircraft equipped with powerful loudspeakers flew high over remote rural villages, broadcasting pre-recorded tapes in Vietnamese that purported to be the voices of the inhabitants' ancestors (rather in the way Robert Duval terrorized peasants by playing Wagner from helicopters in *Apocalypse Now*). The "ancestors" advised their descendants below to have no dealings with the communists and immediately report to the authorities any who might approach them. The thinking behind the strange and spooky scheme was that the average Vietnamese peasant was so backward that he or she would unhesitatingly follow the instructions of their great-great-grandparents even when it was delivered by loudspeakers from flying machines. At the same time, the VC were conducting literacy and political education classes in the same villages.

Organ Transplants

Since the South African surgeon Christiaan Barnard performed the first heart transplant at Cape Town's Groot Schuur Hospital in 1967, the idea that the super-rich might somehow assure themselves of an unlimited supply of replacement organs from living humans has been in constant circulation. A favorite idea is that the healthy but homeless were being kidnapped off the streets and deprived of their hearts, livers, or kidneys and then buried in unmarked graves. A slightly more elaborate horror scenario posed the proposition that Third World "organ farms" were operating in South and Central America. There the potential, albeit scarcely willing donors were being fed and housed in remote jungle compounds until such time as their organs were needed by wealthy customers in the developed countries. A new twist was placed on an old fear by Republican Senator Richard Luger, who, during the 1997 debate on the renewal of China's "most favored nation" trade status, claimed the Chinese government was running a well-established—and highly secret—human spare part industry, selling the organs of political prisoners to a select clientele in Japan and the West.

Ordo Templis Orientis

From around 1900 until at least the late 1960s, the Ordo Templis Orientis (OTO) was something of a minority candidate for the Heart of Darkness. Founded in 1895 by Karl Kellner and Theodore Reuss, OTO was a mystic order of the extreme political right that rejected Christianity and sought the creation of a pan-Germanic world based on pagan spiritual beliefs. As such, it had a profound effect on the coterie of strange individuals who would coagulate to form the core of the fledgling Nazi Party. Before concocting the OTO ideology, both Kellner and Reuss had been powerful **Freemasons**, and Reuss was an officer in the Prussian Secret Service. As the order's membership spread beyond the confines of Germany, its philosophy underwent a degree of mutation to adapt to differing cultural environments. In England, under the leadership of the High Caliph and Great Beast, Aleister Crowley, it took a turn to a ritualistic hedonism more suited to Crowley's own libertine lifestyle.

In the U.S., the branches of the order that flourished in Southern California and on the East Coast from the 1950s well into the 1970s had a grim, apocalyptic view that power, both occult and political, would only be achieved after an Armageddon of a race war. This thinking is believed to have been a serious influence on Charles Manson—Charlie is alleged to have had contact with the OTO Solar Lodge in San Bernardino—and been crucial in the development of his Helter Skelter theories. It is also claimed that the New York–based Son of Sam cult—believed by some to be responsible for the murders for which David Berkowitz was convicted—was conceived from equal parts of OTO and the teachings of the **Process Church** of the Final Judgement.

The most sinister claim regarding OTO is that it attracted many of Col. "Wild Bill" Donovan's first Ivy League recruits, during their college days, to the World War II OSS, the spy network that preceded and spawned the infinitely larger and more powerful **Central Intelligence Agency**. These first contacts infused OTO into the heart of the intelligence community, and ever since, it has been the "house religion" of the upper echelons of the CIA and the model for the creation of mind-control cults like Jim Jones's **People's Temple**.

Otaku

The existence of the obscure Japanese computer-nerd youth movement was originally revealed to western readers in 1995 in the cyberpunk magazine *Wired* and a few months later in the *New York Times*. The Otaku (or more formally, the Otaku-Zoku)—which the most recent estimates figure as over a million strong—are a highly alienated mindset of Japanese youth who turned away from the world and bonded instead with their personal computers. Living in tiny six-mat apartments in Tokyo and other Japanese cities, they exist as virtual shut-ins, losing themselves in an Internet world of e-mail and faxes, swapping gigabytes of pointless but obsessive trivia on manga (the ultra-violent Japanese comic books), monster movies, Japanese pop stars, military hardware, and (believe it or not) tropical fish. At the outer extremes, some Otaku are apparently too uptight to even talk to a phone operator. They find sex with another human a prospect too damaging to think about and have taken mortification of the flesh to such an extreme that they survive on Cup O' Noodles and Slim Fast-style diet products. A few eke out a modest living "road testing" video game modifications and upgrades for Sega, Nintendo, and other software corporations.

Initially, the real world merely shrugged when it learned about the Otaku. The general response was "Okay, so what? At least they stay indoors and don't bother anyone." Then in 1992, one twenty-seven-year-old Otaku, Tsutmo Miyazaki, went on a bizarre **serial killing** spree in the Tokyo dormitory suburb of Hanna, luring pre-teen girls back to his "six mat" where he mutilated and murdered them, carefully logging each grisly move on his computer hard drive. Although the Otaku and their supporters dismiss Miyazaki as an aberration and not typical of the Otaku mainstream, Tokyo police wait watchfully for another outbreak of similar violent detachment from reality.

P

PANDORA

Over the last few years, documents have filtered out under the Freedom of Information Act that refer to a covert Pentagon project code-named PANDORA. Its purpose is to "study the health and psychological effects of low-intensity microwaves" with particular reference to the possibility of creating "auditory hallucinations." These are similar to the voices many paranoid schizophrenics are convinced they hear interpreted as the voice of God giving them instructions or—in the case of **serial killer** David (Son of Sam) Berkowitz—a supernatural dog called Sam. In 1989, a CNN report revealed similar documents indicating plans to field-test various forms of electro-**magnetic** (EM) weapons for use against "terrorists," and that such weapons may have been loaned to either MOSSAD or the Israeli Army to use against rioting Palestinians.

One of the techniques described is acoustic psycho-correction, the "transmission of specific commands via the static or white noise bands in the human subconscious." Known as the Frey Effect, after its discoverer, Alan Frey, such transmissions can create a form of "microwave hearing, a form of artificial telepathy," or to put it another way, another version of the "voice of God" in the subject's head. Further confirmation of this kind of work was provided by ex-US Army Major Edward Dames, who had worked for a PANDORA related psy-tech project known as GRILL FLAME. On an NBC News prime-time TV special, *The Other Side*, broadcast in April of 1995, Dames stated that "the U.S. government has an electronic device which could implant thoughts in people" and that the **CIA** was now working with various sections of law enforcement with a view to it being utilized in situations of "civil unrest, disobedience, and inner-city turmoil created by an increasing impoverished lower class."

The implication in this seems to be that EM weapons have yet to be used in a real confrontation situation, but this again may not be the case. In the 1980s, various women's peace groups set up camp around the USAF air base at Greenham Common in England to protest the presence of American nuclear weapons on British soil. Reports started to come in of protesters suffering from a range of unexplainable symptoms, including "vertigo, retinal bleeding, burnt face, nausea, sleep disturbance, palpitations, loss of concentration and memory, and a sense of panic." In the opinion of Nobel Prize nominee Dr. Robert Becker, all of these effects could have been created if the protesters were being regularly hosed down with low-level EM emissions in an attempt to break their spirit and disrupt their sense of purpose and solidarity. Rumors also persist that EM weaponry was deployed by the FBI at the siege of the **Branch Davidian** compound outside of Waco, Texas, but in the end was never put to use against David Koresh and his followers.

People's Temple, The

The story generally accepted is that the charismatic preacher Jim Jones founded the People's Temple in Ukiah, California, and subsequently moved the congregation to San Francisco, where they formed a powerful political/religious coalition of poor whites and blacks and made important connections to the liberal city administration of Mayor George Moscone and Supervisor Harvey Milk. In the mid-1970s, Jones's mental health started to deteriorate and he may have been using amphetamines. He became increasingly paranoid that the **CIA** was out to get him. In 1977, he moved the entire Temple—with nearly 1,000 followers—to a jungle plantation in the former British colony of Guyana, where he sought to establish a utopian religious commune.

In Guyana, Jones's paranoia grew worse. Rumors of abuse, beatings, and starvation in the Jonestown commune began to filter back to the U.S., and a fact-finding group led by Congressman Leo Ryan went to Jonestown to investigate. This visit is accepted as the final factor that pushed Jones over the edge and convinced him that some kind of biblical apocalypse was at hand. Jones's followers machine-gunned down Ryan and his party as they were leaving Jonestown in two light planes. After these killings, Jones and his followers—913 victims in all—committed mass suicide by drinking Kool-Aid laced with cyanide. The story was horrific, to be sure, but appeared to be a clear example of one more mass freakout by religious extremists.

During the two decades since the alleged mass suicide, some odd facts and a mass of truly nasty conspiracy theories have eased out of the twilight. The Guyanese coroner's report totally contradicted the idea of mass suicide and clearly stated that the majority of victims had either been shot or injected with lethal toxins, and only two committed suicide. Far from being afraid of the CIA, Jones was revealed to have maintained a number of solid links with the agency. He had been personal friends with the agency torture expert, Dan Mitrion, and he had ties with an evangelical media group called World Vision that was later revealed to be a CIA front organization. Even in Guyana, he had been in close touch with other agents at the U.S. embassy in Georgetown. On the other side of the coin, we discover that Congressman Ryan was an outspoken critic of the CIA.

From this point on, the situation becomes weird. Photographs of the body alleged to be that of Jim Jones failed to show some distinctive tattoos. The land in Guyana was leased for Jones by a lawyer who previously worked for the German conglomerate I.G. Farben. (Farben had years earlier held title to the land on which Auschwitz was constructed.) According to an increasing number of authors and Web sites, Jonestown was nothing more than a CIA behavioral experiment, a model for the "**psycho-civilized society**." In what was similar to an experimental concentration camp, "inmates" were observed and tested while being pushed to the limits of physical and psychological stress with drugs supplied by Farben. Sensory deprivation units designed at the Stanford Research Institute numbered among the mind-control hardware. Jones was the CIA's on-site controller, responsible for the continued passivity of the inmates. University of Miami psychologist Jose Lasaga describes Jones's hold on his followers as "mass hypnosis at a social level...a unique process of group regression that led to an acceptance of the leader's delusional system." When leaks about the delusional system began to reach the world media, the experiment was simply and lethally erased, and the cover story of Kool-Aid madness was put into place.

Pfiesteria Pescicida

In the following e-mail communication, fantasy writer Christopher Rowley describes this tiny organism:

> Now we're menaced by things that are almost impossible to pronounce. This is a dinoflagellate, basically algae, that goes into a tiny, alien-like mode (the alien in question is the alien in the Ridley Scott movie *Alien* and its sequels) in the presence of fish—or almost anything edible. It uses a super-toxin to kill the prey that it then devours. It also turns into an amoebal form—microscopic—and can kill or disable people just as easily. Swarms in the polluted estuaries of the world cause huge fish kills. First identified in the 'Hog Waste State', good ol' North Carolina.

Phoenix Program, The

The conflict between the **CIA** and the Vietcong had to be one of the strangest matchings of contenders since Custer and the Seventh Cavalry fought Sitting Bull and the Sioux. The CIA had access to hundreds of millions of dollars, hardware ranging from the B52 bomber to state-of-the-art computers and the ComSat satellite system. The average VC lived on a bowl of rice a day, if need be, and was armed with an AK-47 if he or she was lucky. It seemed to be a conflict of the organic against the machine, and the ultimate outcome had to be the CIA's Phoenix Program, headed by future CIA Director William Colby. The Phoenix Program was the highly ambitious psychological warfare operation that began as part of the effort to win the hearts and minds of the Vietnamese people. It was eventually responsible for the violent deaths of tens of thousands of Vietnamese and the torture of many more. As far as can be ascertained from what records were made public over the years, at least 20,000 suspects died as a result of Phoenix, and some estimates put the number as high as twice that.

The basic concept, because it was largely impossible to differentiate Vietcong agents from the mass of the population, was to set up a network of spies and informers so that the VC could not move through the civilian population, as Chairman Mao Tse Tung said, "like fish through water." It also aimed at convincing VC sympathizers that aiding Charlie was a very bad idea. Many suspects were executed without trial and on little more than the word of an informer. In the process, the CIA all but converted the Republic of Vietnam into a repressive, almost Nazi-style police state. Tough as the Vietcong might have been, the CIA machine's combination of terror and reward—Phoenix operatives would pay as much as $20,000 for a crucial name or piece of information—proved highly effective. Assassination, however, was only one of the wings of the Phoenix. Money and manpower was also poured into a huge campaign of psychological warfare, tactics that would be known ever after as psyops.

Historian Douglas Valentine describes how Phoenix brought its psyop campaign into play: "Because fear of the Phoenix Program was an effective means of creating informers and defectors, an intensive publicity campaign called "The Popular Information Program" was instituted. Psychological warfare teams crisscrossed the country using Phoenix supplied radios, leaflets, posters, TV shows, movies, banners, and even loudspeakers mounted on sampans to get the message across."

The message was a simple one—"root out the evil commies i midst." In many respects, the CIA were fighting in Vietnam for mor the obvious objective of defeating the Vietcong. Vietnam provided the perfect test bed for weapons that waited in readiness through most of the Cold War. Everything from Claymore mines to defoliants like Agent Orange could be put through their paces under full-combat conditions. In the case of the CIA's psyop techniques, Vietnam was the culmination of experimental programs by ultra-secret research sections like **MKULTRA** and would become the model for future operations in Central America.

Philadelphia Experiment, The

The Philadelphia Experiment is one of the great technological legends to emerge from World War II. Debate over the details of the story and whether it really happened or is just an elaborate piece of disinformation continues to this day. In brief, the story is that the U.S. Navy, in October of 1943, attempted to make a destroyer, the USS *Eldridge* (D-17), invisible both to the naked eye and to radar. The method used attempted to bend light around the vessel by the use of a massively powerful **magnetic** field. Much of the background research that went into the system was apparently based on Albert Einstein's Unified Field Theory and the work of **Nikola Tesla**.

The first test involving the *Eldridge* allegedly was to see if it could be made invisible to the naked eye, and most versions of the story seem to agree that this was a relative success. According to witnesses from a nearby Liberty ship, the SS *Andrew Furuseth*, the *Eldridge* was enveloped in what looked like a green mist. After some seconds, the mist dissipated and the *Eldridge* completely vanished, leaving what looked like a flat, untroubled sea. A few moments later the process reversed itself, the mist reappeared, and this time when it faded, the destroyer was back again. The crew who had been onboard during this period of invisibility complained of feeling groggy and disorientated as the same green mist that had been seen by distant observers filled the entire ship and seemed to completely envelope them. Afterwards, though, they showed no lasting ill effects.

A second test, on the other hand, did not run as smoothly. The objective this time was to render the *Eldridge* undetectable by radar, and the magnetic field was made even more powerful. The *Eldridge* vanished much in the way it had before, only this time it left a well-defined impression of its hull in the water. When it returned, the experiment was immediately seen to have had a horrific and disastrous effect on the crew. Some had vanished, others were incinerated, a few mangled bodies had actually been fused into the metal of the ship, and the majority of those who remained physically intact were incoherent. If what happened to the men wasn't bad enough, alarmed reports came from miles away in Norfolk, Virginia. The *Eldridge* suddenly appeared in the ocean off Norfolk and then, just as suddenly, vanished again. The only inference that could be placed on these events was that somehow the magnetic fields used to camouflage the *Eldridge* had done much more. They instantly teleported it the few hundred miles from its base in the Philadelphia Naval Yard to the sea near Norfolk. Aside from the fact that it looked impossible for human beings to come through the process intact, the problem was that no one had the slightest idea of how it could be controlled.

In a third and final experiment, the *Eldridge* was again subjected to the magnetic field but this time with no crew aboard. As on the previous two occasions, it vanished and reappeared again, but no reports came back of it appearing elsewhere. Instead, this time a major part of the equipment that generated the magnetic field had inexplicably vanished when it came back. At this point the Navy supposedly dropped the whole idea. Either because the line of research had turned into an embarrassment or perhaps, with the Manhattan Project to develop the atom bomb getting underway, there may have been a conflict of available funding.

The Philadelphia Experiment didn't die with this supposed official cancellation. It lived on in contemporary folklore. Stories endured of survivors of the second experiment who continued to randomly vanish and reappear again, placing intolerable strain on their already stressed minds. Two crewmen who apparently panicked and jumped overboard during the disappearance phase of the second experiment were supposed to have found themselves stranded in Montauk, New York, in 1983. Somehow, the idea of magnetism being the key to the secret of teleportation and movement through space, in a way that transcended the physical laws as laid out by Einstein, connected the Philadelphia Experiment with concepts like time travel, the Bermuda Triangle, and even UFOs. The possibility has also been mooted that the idea wasn't dropped before the end of World War II, but continues today inside ultra-secret facilities like **Area 51**.

Phone Taps

Graffiti on a New York City pay phone—"Don't call that 800 number that tells you if your phone's tapped. They'll tap your phone."

Pine Gap

Pine Gap is starting to qualify, in the realm of conspiracists, as Australia's **Area 51**. The highly secret base is just twelve miles from the town of Alice Springs in Australia's Northern Territory. It is presented to the world as a "Joint Defense Research Facility" shared by the U.S. and the Australians. But it has always been assumed to really be a **National Security Agency** download link for spy satellites like SIGNIT that remain in geosynchronous orbit over various parts of the Earth. An Australian university professor, who understandably wishes to remain nameless, reveals that perhaps more than just satellite monitoring may be going on in the outback. On an all-night hunting trip near Pine Gap, he and three reliable companions witnessed a camouflaged door open up in the grounds of the base and a circular metallic disc, very similar to the classic flying saucer, rise vertically then head away at great speed. This and other similar reports have led to a spate of antipodean rumors that Pine Gap has become another site of human/alien collaboration.

Plum Island

Plum Island, off the north fork of New York's Long Island, is famous among military black operations theorists. The place is forbidden territory to the media or anyone else and has long been thought to be the center of bacterial research that includes biological warfare. In the 1990s, a number of particle accelerators were constructed on the island and are clearly visible from the air. The current theory is that Plum Island is being used as a center for research on the effects of particle beams on human genetic material. In crude terms, we may have death ray experiments going on just two hours from New York City.

Plum Island surfaced in popular fiction when, in the book and movie *The Silence of the Lambs*, Hannibal Lecter, the genius **serial killer**, was offered a home there by FBI Agent Clarice Starling.

Plutonium

Rumors abound about how a sophisticated black market in the former Soviet Union is selling and exporting weapon-grade plutonium just like cocaine out of Colombia, but few truly care to speculate about just how much of this dangerous and truly obscene metal is currently in circulation. Most reports that have surfaced, notably on the TV show *60 Minutes* and in the *New York Times* and the *Washington Post*, would indicate that black market plutonium is averaging about $150,000 per kilogram. Bootleg bomb components are offered for sale by impoverished ex-Soviet scientists in a similar price range. With prices that deep in the bargain basement, it would be theoretically possible for a medium-sized coke cartel, fanatic terror cell, or even some mad capitalist billionaire to own an A-bomb or two of their very own. The grim fact also remains that one doesn't even need a nuclear device to wipe out a major city. A simple suitcase containing a few pounds of plutonium jacketed around a charge of C4 or even old-fashioned dynamite is more than enough. Detonate something like that in Times Square, Picadilly Circus, or the Ginza and New York, London, or Tokyo would be rendered uninhabitable for hundreds of thousands of years.

Political Advertising

Political TV commercials are the only form of advertising specifically exempt from truth in advertising regulations by the Federal Communications Commission as protected speech under the First Amendment.

Porno Addiction

If the economic numbers provide any guide, according to the *Sunday Times* of London, America is in the grip of a major pornography addiction. The adult entertainment industry in the U.S. now generates over $10 billion a year. Rentals of porno films now account for more than 25 percent of the entire videocassette market, while the income from strip clubs exceeds that of all other live entertainment combined, including theatre and rock concerts. No longer is the porno industry the sleazy, backroom enterprise that many imagine it to be. Major corporations have moved into the area, such as AT&T, which provides lines and 900 numbers for phone sex, and Time-Warner, which now owns a hardcore, cable-TV sex channel.

Presley, Elvis

For approximately the first fifteen years after the death of Elvis Presley, crazy rumors spread like wildfire. Elvis was alive, having faked his own death. Elvis would return when the time was right. Elvis was haunting the pool house at Graceland. The London *Daily Mirror* claimed that Elvis had been hit by the Mafia after a deal made on a private jet once owned by fugitive financier Robert Vesco went wrong. A strange, punk urban legend claimed that Elvis's body had been ground to hamburger, sold by the pound, and eaten in a ceremonial ritual by the likes of Bruce Springsteen and Mick Jagger. A whole subgenre of paranormal Elvis stories kept the supermarket tabloids in lurid front covers for months, and Elvis sightings proliferated like glimpses of Bigfoot in a national park. Elvis was even reported peering from the window of a UFO. Writer Gail Brewer Giorgio parlayed her theories that Elvis was alive into a book and two syndicated TV specials. A strange quasi-religion started to form around his memory.

Although the religious overtones remain, the Elvis rumors have slowed to a minor trickle. Elvis has left the auditorium and gone to his reward. He will definitely not be back, and the only conspiracy theory attached to his death is that Colonel Tom Parker and officials at Baptist Memorial Hospital may have made some moves to conceal the true (and truly awesome) extent of Elvis's multiple-drug habit. They were reasonably successful until Geraldo Rivera blew the story wide open on a 1979 edition of the TV show *20/20,* entitled "The Elvis Cover-Up."

Two things have never been explained. First, during the final 1977 concert tour before his death, Elvis made a habit of moving to the front of the stage and whispering the words, "I am and I was" to the front rows of the audience. Why? Second, although Elvis took out a multimillion-dollar insurance policy a short time before he died, why has none of his family tried to claim it?

Prisoner, The

If the TV series **The X-Files** is an accurate representation of prevailing paranoia in the 1990s, the show *The Prisoner* certainly did much the same for the 1960s. The brainchild of its star, actor Patrick McGoohan, the series followed the adventures of a James Bond-style British secret agent known simply as Number Six. After attempting to quit the service, he discovers not only that is he unable to resign but that he is drugged and incarcerated in a bizarre and highly psychedelic leisure complex called The Village. The complex is a place where ex-agents from both sides in the Cold War are confined, regimented, and brainwashed on a permanent vacation. The Village is guarded by huge and deadly robot balloons ("rovers") that smother any prisoner who crosses the defined perimeter. Just to add to the sense of **Kafka**-like unreality, the sequences in The Village were shot in a real place, Portmerion, a strange tourist resort on Cardigan Bay in North Wales. Portmerion was previously a popular retreat for individuals like Noël Coward, George Bernard Shaw, and of course, Patrick McGoohan.

The Prisoner, which ran on **CBS** during the 1968 and 1969 seasons, was assumed by most fans to be a somewhat weird sequel to the 1965 show *Secret Agent,* in which McGoohan played another Bond-clone, John Drake. The fans also believed its intention was to prove that the intelligence business was far more dangerously weird than Ian Fleming had ever suggested. Each episode followed Number Six's attempts to escape from The Village and generally thwart the attempts of his nameless and mysterious captors to mess with his mind. Although it generated critical acclaim and a huge cult following among hippies and conspiracy theorists that survives to this day, the show proved too left-field for an American audience and was cancelled after seventeen episodes. It is regularly rerun on various cable channels and is available on commercial videocassette.

Private Jet Fighters

For the man who literally has everything, how about his very own high-performance jet fighter aircraft? Although the U.S. Air Force breaks up its decommissioned planes for scrap, the new cash-strapped republics of the former Soviet Union have no reservations about selling off their surplus military hardware, even to private citizens. Prices range from $50,000 to $400,000 and as of 1998, some 423 Americans have put down the bucks and are now the proud owners of a Russian MiG-29 or a Czech L-39. Although the armaments are stripped from the aircraft, owners can still perform Top Gun-style maneuvers at twice the speed of sound. Comments Allen Smith, the company vice president, who owns an L-39: "It's better than sex."

Process Church, The

The Process Church of the Final Judgement was first established in London's upmarket Mayfair area in 1967—the so-called Summer of Love. Its members, with their long, Christ-like, center-parted hair and uniform black and purple capes, quickly became a familiar sight at psychedelic clubs and hippie gatherings. They seemed very keen on recruiting bikers and hippies to their movement, particularly wealthy hippies and—best of all—wealthy, hippie rock stars. In this, they were less than successful. According to legend, they had a stoned Marianne Faithfull in their clutches for a few days, but she was ultimately rescued by some burly Rolling Stones' roadies and bodyguards. Their philosophy was that good and evil—symbolized by Jesus and Lucifer—were simply the two sides of the same yin/yang coin. It may have had a certain appeal if it hadn't conjured such loud echoes of Aleister Crowley's "do what you will is the only law" and if their logo hadn't been too similar to a Nazi swastika redrawn by a slick Swiss typographer.

It was only with the publication of *The Family*, Ed Sanders's 1971 gonzo account of Charlie Manson and his followers, that we started to discover what The Process was really about. Even that was rendered sketchy by the removal of a crucial chapter of the book after threats of a massive lawsuit by **The Church of Scientology**. The essential thread seemed to be that Robert DeGrimston, a breakaway Scientologist, who founded The Process in 1963 as a money-spinning, mind-control entity, experienced some kind of dark epiphany in Xtul in the Yucatan. After that, things swerved a little out of hand—some claimed that The Process and the Manson Family committed a number of joint ritual murders, possibly in the name of Abraxus, the rooster-headed Gnostic god in whom darkness and light are both united and transcended. DeGrimston's wife, Kathy, also didn't help matters by claiming to be a reincarnation of Joseph Goebbels and Hecate. By 1974, The Process had dropped off the radar.

Or so we thought.

And then in 1996, a Process Web site appeared on the Internet, and the February 1997 issue of *Alternative Press* magazine ran a feature detailing both the history and the return of the Process—without Robert DeGrimston. It described how the newly revived cult had an influence on a number of alternative rockers, most notably the band Skinny Puppy. The Web site and the *Alternative Press* article were both vague regarding the aims and beliefs of this resuscitated but seemingly sanitized Process. Both appeared to confirm that the 1960s, both good and bad, are always with us.

Project HAARP

Up in Gakona, in the Alaskan wilderness, lurks a secret installation—an underground facility of indeterminate size surmounted by a forest of tall, spindly antennae. The installation is known as HAARP, an acronym for High-Frequency Active **Aurora** Research Project. Although operated and funded by the Air Force in conjunction with the Navy, HAARP hardly looks or sounds like a super-weapon. The Pentagon claims its only purpose is to conduct research into electro**magnetic** (EM) phenomena in the upper atmosphere, but it has a lot of people worried. One of the worried is "black world investigator" Mark Farmer. His fears were aired in a chat session on the *Sightings* Web site in June 1996: "In its present form, it's not a weapon . . . yet. A more powerful HAARP could fry a spaceship in orbit and be very handy in detecting stealth vehicles and boosting communication capabilities. An even more powerful system could, in theory, change the weather and alter brain chemistry."

What concerns Farmer more is that, even taking Project HAARP on its face value statement that it will be conducting experiments on the ionosphere and Aurora phenomenon, it could trigger a gruesome and global environmental disaster. "We don't quite know what the ionosphere does. Some scientists refer to it as the: 'ignorosphere.' We blew nukes up in it, and now HAARP will punch holes in it and cut slices out of it. We'll find out soon enough." Quite possibly at a terrible cost. Like the already ragged ozone layer, the ionosphere may protect us from all manner of lethal stuff from space.

A number of HAARP critics take this a stage further and state that the advertised ionosphere research is nothing more than a cover for a new ground-based phase of the **Reagan** era Strategic Defense Initiative (SDI)—the Star Wars program. Among the most vociferous is Dr. Nicholas Beglich, who has been actively monitoring HAARP transmissions. He claims his research has revealed a group of EM emissions in the 435 MHz range. He reasons that because the frequency window of human consciousness is supposedly in the area of 400-450 MHz, some of HAARP's more covert objectives are actually in the realm of mind control. These signals of 400–450 MHz are seemingly capable of resonating neutrons in the human brain and directly affecting the mental processes. The HAARP broadcasts could be bounced back to Earth, via the small SDI "popcorn" satellites in orbit since the late 1980s, and the effects on human beings recorded as preliminary research into the ultimate possibility of creating that longed for **psycho-civilized society**.

Protocols of the Elders of Zion, The

The Protocols of the Elders of Zion was possibly one of the most destructive forgeries in history, leading as it did almost directly to the Nazi holocaust. Supposedly a secret account of a meeting of the World Congress of Jewry held in Basel, Switzerland, in 1897, it detailed a conspiracy by the international Jewish movement, with the aid of the **Freemasons**, to achieve world domination. Smuggled into Germany at the beginning of World War I by the ultra-secret, right-wing **Thule Society**, it became the documentary basis for twentieth-century anti-Semitism, and Hitler incorporated much of its content into his political thesis *Mein Kampf*. Even when *The Protocols* were proved to be a forgery perpetrated by dissident members of the Czarist secret police, many right-wingers still treated them as the genuine article and used them as a foundation for their hate campaigns. You might think that after a hundred years, the poison would have dissipated, but the sad truth is they continue to be dragged out by fascists and anti-Semites. If you don't believe this, pick up some neo-Nazi literature or stop by your nearest Aryan Brotherhood meeting.

Psilocybin

In an interview with *Mondo 2000*, magazine lecturer and psychedelic guru Terence McKenna cast a whole new light on the drug psilocybin, the magic mushroom used in hippie mind expansion and Native American religious ceremonies. "There are alien traces on this planet and perhaps alien artifacts, and maybe psychedelic molecules *are* alien artifacts...Psilocybin is 4-phosphoryloxy-N, N-DMT. It's the only 4-substituted indole on this planet...it indicates it's from outside the terrestrial environment. Or it was designed. If you talk to evolutionary biologists, one of the ways they talk about an organism is to equate evolutionary progress with energetic efficiency. You look at psilocybin mushrooms—15–20 percent of the metabolic energy is going into the production of psilocybin. And psilocybin is not something the mushrooms have to have.

"The psilocybin receptor in the brain is the cerebellum receptor itself, which is the major system that we're running on, that all life is running on. You can find serotonin in organisms clear down to the flatworm. As you ascend the phylogeny, the amount of serotonin increases. Primates have more serotonin in them than any other organisms and human beings have more serotonin than any other primates. Clearly, if there is a marker for consciousness, serotonin is it. Now, psilocybin directly competes with serotonin. It seems to me that when we understand what memory storage and recall and all this sort of thing actually is, then psilocybin will be seen to be very obviously the equivalent of a radio. It's a nanotechnological radio built by a nanotech, biotech, sophisticated civilization of some sort. When you turn it on, you don't hear about your childhood trauma, you hear weather reports from Betelgeuse and all of the rest of the stuff that's coming through there."

Kinda puts a new slant on turning on and tuning in, doesn't it?

Psycho-Civilized Society

The idea of total control of a population—be it of a country, continent, religious group, or the entire planet—has been the dream of popes, princes, kings, mullahs, and dictators probably for as long as human beings have lived in any kind of organized community. "Wouldn't life be so much easier if everyone thought like I do, acted like I do, and did exactly what they were told without question?" The means used to achieve this state of mass passivity and total obedience have varied from inflexible religious dogma enforced by fear of torture and execution to political brainwashing maintained by a lockstep police state where every move the citizen made was carefully monitored. Both Stalin and Hitler sought to create the ideal of the New Man, the individual who, via cradle-to-grave propaganda, conditioning, and thought control, could be deprived of all individualism and freewill and whose loyalty to the state and its leaders would be automatic, unquestioned, and permanent.

Although the term "psycho-civilized society" had yet to be coined, George Orwell speculated on exactly that in his novel *1984*. Mao Tse Tung may have attempted something of the kind when he let loose the Red Guard during China's Cultural Revolution of the mid-1960s. It was certainly what Pol Pot and the Khmer Rouge tried to achieve in the next decade with the mass slaughter on the killing fields of Cambodia, as they worked to destroy all vestiges of previous society in their horrific Year Zero programs. The idea of the psycho-civilized society in its current form has certainly been around since the establishment of the **CIA**'s **MKULTRA** program in 1953, when Research Director Sid Gottlieb toyed with the concept of subduing entire populations by using drugs, mass hypnosis, or other means.

In the last decade, new ultra-high-tech methods of creating this kind of human social anthill have started, bit by bit, to come to light. Writing for the Web site *Parascope*, English researcher David G. Guyatt notes that government agencies in both the U.S. and Europe currently possess "innovative technological weapons that do not necessarily kill but could render disfranchised segments of society physically inactive, emotionally stupefied, and incapable of meaningful thought."

This new arsenal of weapons certainly includes such modern miracles of black science as direct brain stimulation, mind alteration by the use of extra-low-frequency microwave emissions, and radio hypnosis. (All of these are examined in greater detail in other parts of this book.) It also includes other more advanced systems that may yet come to light. In all cases, the target is the human brain. If minds can be controlled, all else should logically follow. Torture, threat, and the ever-present secret police would hardly be needed. Trip a switch or press a button and free will becomes history.

Unfortunately, what would logically follow would be the most absolute form of totalitarianism imaginable, with a small, hidden power elite controlling a human anthill completely unable to think for itself. The psycho-civilized society would be, as they used to say in those 1950s, black-and-white horror movies, "the end of civilization as we know it." Humanity may be a quarrelsome, overpopulating mess here at the dawn of the twenty-first century, but it is, at least, our very own mess and not a mindless quasi-utopia where every aspect of life is planned out for us by politicians, the heads of multinational corporations, or some other shadowy wannabe dictatorship. We will either solve our current problems or we won't. What the human race doesn't need is for the ability to solve problems—and on the other side of the coin, to screw up royally—to be nullified and negated by men, women, and children being uniformly drugged, wired, implanted, or bombarded with electrons. Regrettably, small but determined groups of men and women still don't agree with the preceding statement and apparently continue to work toward the goal of control as though it were the cure for all our ills.

Pumpkin Seed

Along with the **Aurora** spyplane, the Pumpkin Seed is another class of super-secret terrestrial aircraft that may be mistaken for UFOs over **Area 51** in Nevada. The Pumpkin Seed's propulsion system involves igniting fuel outside the body of the craft in a series of pulses that produce opposing shock waves that shoot the craft forward at hypersonic speed. It works by exerting pressure on the plane's flattened, diamond-shaped body from above and below, rather like squeezing a pumpkin seed between the thumb and index finger. The igniting fuel is alleged to produce bright flashes of light when the craft is in flight and may be the cause of some Area 51 UFO reports.

Q

Quayle, J. Danforth

In 1988, when Dan Quayle was running for election as George Bush's vice president, a potentially damaging piece of information almost came to light that could have wrecked the ultra-conservative's political prospects. In mid-October, a matter of weeks before the nation went to the polls, a federal prisoner named Brett Kimberlin, doing time at the El Reno Correctional Facility for drug smuggling, issued a statement to the press that he sold **marijuana** to Dan Quayle "fifteen to twenty times" when the future VP was a law student in Indianapolis in the early 1970s. Kimberlin volunteered to undergo a polygraph test and claimed that he would go into details of the charges at a press conference later in the same month.

To say the allegations caused consternation among Republicans is an understatement. Quayle was already suffering from the public perception that he was a lightweight rich kid who had no business being "a heartbeat away from the presidency." For it to come out that he had been a student pothead, when the "War on Drugs" was one of the major planks of the Bush/Quayle platform, was potentially devastating. Fortunately for Quayle, the press conference never happened. Four days before the election, Bureau of Prisons Director Michael Quinlan—a **Reagan** political appointee—contacted the warden at El Reno and told him the Kimberlin press conference should be cancelled. Less than an hour before the conference was due to take place, Kimberlin himself was tossed into solitary where he remained until eight days after the election.

When the story surfaced in the *New York Times* and the *San Francisco Examiner*, David Beckwith, a Quayle spokesperson, dismissed the entire incident: "This belongs in the comics pages." Accordingly, Gary Trudeau devoted a number of episodes of his *Doonesbury* strip to the Dan Quayle reefer story.

R

Ramirez, Gloria

After Gloria Ramirez died of cancer in 1994 at Riverside General Hospital in Riverside, California, weird toxic fumes emanated from her body, and a number of emergency workers who had been exposed to her collapsed or became seriously ill. No explanation has ever been offered by authorities as to the cause of this bizarre event, but rumors are rife that the thirty-one-year-old Ramirez belonged to an alien-abductee or ritual-abuse support group.

Reagan, Ronald (1)

During a special screening at the White House of **Steven Spielberg**'s popular film *ET*, Ronald Reagan amazed those present by remarking to the ace Hollywood director, who must have been amazed himself, "There are probably only six people in this room who know how true this all is."

Reagan, Ronald (2)

Writing in the *New York Times* in 1987, historian C. Vann Woodward revealed that while president of the Screen Actors Guild in the early 1950s, the future president was a regular FBI informer, and that Reagan "fed the names of suspect people in his organization to the FBI secretly and regularly enough to be assigned an informer's code number, T-10."

REX 84

In July 1984, the Knight-Ridder news service broke the story of REX 84. Devised in the basement of the **Reagan** White House by Oliver North and National Guard Colonel Louis Giuffrida, REX 84 was a plan to "crush national opposition to any military action abroad" by "the suspension of the Constitution and the turning of control of the government over to **FEMA**." According to columnist Jack Anderson, it also called for the "internment in concentration camps of up to 100,000 illegal immigrants and political dissidents" and would "clamp Americans in a totalitarian vice."

The seeds for REX 84 had originally been planted during the Kennedy administration, when Executive Order 11051 provided for the temporary suspension of the Constitution and a declaration of martial law in the event of nuclear attack. The order was rewritten during the administration of Richard Nixon to make the same sort of action possible in a large number of national emergencies including civil insurrections. Finally North and Giuffrida expanded and redefined the order so that it could be enacted at the sole discretion of the president or any designated surrogate. Although the Iran-Contra investigations uncovered and sidetracked REX 84, its legal underpinnings still remain on the books. In the estimation of Professor Diana Reynolds of Northeastern University, "America is only a presidential directive away from a civil security state of emergency."

RHIC-EDOM

Since the early 1980s, dozens of pieces of information have floated to the surface that indicated that the quest for technological mind control is alive and kicking. One tantalizing bit of data came from a former FBI agent, Lincoln Lawrence, who revealed the existence of a 350-page **CIA** document outlining a technique with the convoluted acronym RHIC-EDOM—Radio Hypnosis Intra-Cerebral Control-Electronic Dissolution of Memory. RHIC-EDOM appears to be either an evolution or an outgrowth of the experiments in the 1950s where electrodes were implanted in the brains of rats, other animals, and possibly human subjects that could provoke extreme emotions: "rage, lust, fatigue, etc." The apparent leap forward made by RHIC-EDOM was that instead of hardwiring the actual brain, similar effects—particularly those of disorientation and loss of memory—could be achieved by various forms of electronic bombardment by radio and microwaves.

Roaches

As comedian Richard Belzer once remarked—"Only rats, roaches, and Keith Richards will survive a nuclear war."

Rogers, Charles Frederick

As over the years, more and more shadowy figures are added to the list of possible suspects in the **Kennedy assassination**, the somewhat unfortunately named Fred Rogers is possibly one of the most bizarre to be dragged out of the murk. Rogers was identified by Houston police forensic artist Lois Gibson as "Frenchy," the shortest of the "three tramps" apprehended in Dealey Plaza, found hiding in a railroad car behind the grassy knoll but subsequently and mysteriously let go. (Many conspiracists and assassination researchers identify the other two as E. Howard Hunt of

Watergate fame and **Charles Harrelson**, the father of movie star Woody Harrelson. They charge them as the hit men—one of the three teams positioned around Dealey Plaza—shooting at JFK from behind the picket fence in the grassy knoll area.)

As if being a suspect in one of the major JFK conspiracy theories wasn't enough of a criminal claim to fame, Rogers goes one better. He is the sole suspect in the murder of his father and mother in their home in Houston on Father's Day 1965. The murder was a particularly gruesome one, with the couple butchered and dismembered and the mother's head placed in the crisper of the family refrigerator. Rogers disappeared immediately after the killings and was declared legally dead in 1975. Private detective John R. Craig thinks otherwise. At the 1991 JFK Assassination Symposium in Dallas, Craig alleged how Rogers worked for the **CIA** since 1956, had been a personal friend of David Ferrie, another major assassination suspect, and like Ferrie, had been in the Civil Air Patrol. In Craig's scenario, far from being dead, Fred Rogers was spirited out of Texas to South America by a CIA plane, where he continued to work for the agency right through to the Iran-Contra program, during which he piloted transport aircraft for **Air America**.

Romania

After the overthrow of evil Romanian dictator Nicolae Ceausescu, the liberating mob that broke into the Bucharest headquarters of his feared secret police made a surprising discovery. For years, it was assumed that most of the telephones in the country, if not tapped, were open to eavesdropping at a moment's notice. As it turned out, the secret police only had sufficient technology to tap a few dozen telephones at any one time. Big Brother, it seemed, was mainly in the ear of the beholder. In fact, this does make logical sense. If everyone in a police state were watched constantly, even with the watchers working twelve-hour shifts, two-thirds of the population would be constantly employed in watching the other one-third. Clearly, tyrannies need to generate a considerable level of paranoia to maintain their control.

Roswell

For most practical purposes, the events in the small town of Roswell, New Mexico, provided the seed from which all contemporary alien conspiracy theories have grown. The legend, as handed down by UFO buffs, is as follows: In July of 1947, a flying disc of unearthly origin supposedly crashed during a violent thunderstorm seventy miles northwest of Roswell. Debris was discovered by Mac Brazel, a local rancher, who after a day or so of delay, drove into the town of Roswell and reported the find to Sheriff George A. Wilcox. Wilcox, in turn, contacted the military at the nearby the Roswell Army Air Field, home to the 509th Bomb Group of the Eighth Air Force. After Air Force personnel surrounded and sealed the crash site and hauled a considerable quantity of debris back to the base, the Roswell Army Air Base Public Information Officer, First Lieutenant Walter G. Haut, issued the proud statement that the U.S. Army Air Force was in possession of the remains of a genuine flying saucer. What has become known as the "Roswell Statement" was as follows:

> The many rumors regarding the flying disc became a reality yesterday when the intelligence office of the 509th Bomb Group of the Eighth Air Force was fortunate enough to gain possession of a disc through the cooperation of one of the local ranchers and the sheriff's office of Chaves County.
>
> The flying object landed on a ranch near Roswell sometime last week. Not having phone facilities, the rancher stored the disc until such time as he was able to contact the sheriff's office, which in turn notified Major Jesse A. Marcel of the 509th Bomb Group intelligence office.
>
> Action was immediately taken and the disc was picked up at the rancher's home. It was inspected at the Roswell Army Airfield and subsequently loaned to higher headquarters by Major Marcel.

For the next twenty-four hours, as Haut's statement went out to the world via radio, wire services, and news agencies, Roswell became the storm center of a global sensation. Finally, the U.S. military was going to reveal the truth behind all those pesky saucer sightings that had been causing so much speculation and had reached an all-time peak in June of 1947. And then, amazingly, the Army Air Force did a complete about face. No, the story was all wrong. A stupid mistake had been made. No crashed flying saucer had been recovered at all. The debris discovered by the rancher was nothing more than the remains of a downed radar target balloon. In order that nothing should challenge this account, reporters' notes were confiscated, Mac Brazel was held incommunicado for over a week, the Roswell area was sealed off by the military, and an embarrassed-looking Major Marcel confronted the press with what was obviously the remains of a mundane terrestrial balloon.

If the military's intention had been to quiet the speculation and put a stop to the stories that they found a UFO, they couldn't have done a more botched job. For the next half-century, the stories surrounding the Roswell incident expanded in both extent and complexity. The debris discovered by Mac Brazel was only part of the picture. More debris, bodies, and perhaps a live alien were discovered at a second site nearer to Corona, New Mexico. The bodies and debris were flown to Wright Field (now Wright Patterson Air Force Base) near Dayton, Ohio, where they were stored in the notorious Hangar 18. The **Majestic 12** group was set up to coordinate dealing with the alien problem and reporting back to the president. In the more extreme scenarios, the aliens themselves arrive in force and begin a covert takeover of the Earth. On the fiftieth anniversary of the Roswell Incident, the Air Force weighed in with its own bizarre contribution to the event—what they claimed was a "final report." They stated that any bodies that might have been seen around the crash site were maybe crash test dummies attached to the radar target balloon. In an odd postscript, in 1978, while supposedly suffering from lung cancer, Jesse Marcel reconfirmed in interviews that the debris at Roswell was not of this Earth.

One aspect of the Roswell legend that cannot be refuted is that on the strength of all the stories, theories, and legends, Roswell, New Mexico now has a UFO museum and a thriving, somewhat unexpected tourist industry.

S

Sangumas

It is usually assumed that the hired hit man, if not a modern phenomenon, is at least the product of a reasonably evolved culture. In the remote highlands of Papua New Guinea, however, where inhabitants have hardly advanced beyond the level of the Stone Age, a cult of medicine men known as sangumas will also commit murder for a price. These homicidal witch doctors, who are usually paid in livestock and trinkets, have a unique method of avoiding detection and disposing of their victims. After the hit has been carried out, the killers eat the body of the victim.

Satanic UFOs

Since the start of the UFO sighting phenomenon, fundamentalist Christians have been unable to make up their minds where they stand on the matter, gradually coming to a semi-official belief that UFOs are the work of the Devil. As early as 1980, a fundamentalist tract titled *The Cult Explosion* by David

Hunt stated, "UFOs...are clearly not physical and seem to be demonic manifestations from another dimension calculated to alter man's way of thinking...[they] are demons and they are preparing for the **Antichrist**."

Hal Lindsey, in his 1994 religious best seller, *Planet Earth—2000 A.D.*, echoes the same sentiment: "I have become thoroughly convinced that UFOs are real . . . to be blunt, I think they are part of a Satanic plot."

School of the Americas

The use of torture has been largely outlawed by most civilized countries as being both morally repugnant and practically ineffective. The former hardly needs any clarification, and the latter is neatly summed up in a **CIA** document from the early 1950s that condemns the use of torture because of its "dubious effectiveness as compared with various supplemental psychoanalytical techniques." Or as one field operative more bluntly put it, "You can blowtorch a man's ass, but he'll only tell you what you want to hear." Despite these reservations, evidence abounds that the CIA more than once applied the metaphoric blowtorch and the not so metaphoric bullet in the back of the head. They even taught the more refined techniques of murder and torture to military and law enforcement officials of client countries, first at the International Police Academy in Los Fresnos, Texas, and later at the notorious School of the Americas at Fort Benning, Georgia.

The curriculum at the School of the Americas—essentially based on the brutal but relatively effective **Phoenix Program** used in Vietnam but modified for primary use in Latin America—provides an horrific blueprint for the conversion of any medium-sized nation into a ruthlessly aggressive police state by means of repression, intimidation, and execution. One of its primary textbooks that has become public in recent years is *The CIA Interrogation Manual*. Although the book concentrates on the psychological techniques for breaking down a subject, it is implicit that the described intimidation and disorientation may be used—in combination with drugs—as adjuncts to physical torture such as beating, burning, electric shock, partial drowning, sleep deprivation, and rape.

"The ideal time to make an arrest is in the early hours of the morning. When arrested at this time, most subjects experience intense feelings of shock, insecurity, and psychological stress." As arrest moves to incarceration and actual questioning, the instructions in the manual become increasingly grim. "The subject must be convinced that his 'questioner' controls his ultimate destiny and that his absolute cooperation is necessary for his survival." That the manual sees the psychological softening up only as a prelude to worse suffering is hardly disguised. "A threat should be delivered coldly, not shouted in anger. When a threat is used, it should always be implied that the subject himself is to blame. 'You leave me no other choice but to...' If a subject refuses to comply after a threat is made, it must be carried out. If it is not carried out, then other threats become meaningless."

A second manual—issued to the Nicaraguan Contras under the title *The CIA Freedom Fighters' Manual*—goes a step further and covers the subject of death squads. It stresses that the fiction must be maintained that a death squad—a murder unit with the specific task of eliminating suspected political undesirables, usually composed of either off-duty police or military personnel—has no visible connection with the ruling authority. At the same time, however, it has to be known that it was the fatal vengeance of that same authority that instigated the killings. In Vietnam, the Phoenix squads left ace of spades calling cards beside the bodies of their suspected VC victims. Under various Latin American regimes, the death squads make themselves known by driving a particular make and model of car. In the 1960s, the Ford Falcon was the car of choice, but by the 1980s, it had been replaced by the Jeep Cherokee. In El Salvador, the death squads of Roberto D'Aubuisson wore black Oakland Raiders T-shirts as unofficial uniforms.

In the Spring 1994 edition of *Covert Action Quarterly*, writer Clyde Snow describes how the CIA School of the Americas trained death squads operated in Guatemala during the 1970s and 1980s: "An informer with a hooded face accompanies police along a city street, pointing people out: who shall live and who shall die... 'this one's a son of a bitch'... 'that one'... anyone with the vaguely leftist political association or moderate criticism of government policy. Men (are) found with their eyes gouged out, their testicles in their mouths, without hands or tongues, women with their breasts cut off." If it starts to sound as though the School of the Americas is a training ground for homicidal sadists, Clyde Snow leaves us in no doubt, "The military guys who do this are like **serial killers**. If Jeffrey Dahmer had been in Guatemala, he would be a general by now."

Secret Societies

No one likes a secret society. They are spooky, they do stuff that no else is allowed to know about. They treat the rest of the world as outsiders and operate according to hidden agendas that may not take into account the comfort and welfare of you and me. Worst of all, no one knows exactly who they are. The **Freemasons**, for example, are reputed to include among their membership most of the world's power elite. The truth is, of course, that secret societies sponsoring a multitude of sins range from the **Bavarian Illuminati**, who are reputed to run everything, to Ralph Kramden's Raccoon Lodge, which was inevitably and consistently a couple of sandwiches short of a picnic.

Seekers after Truth

"There's a seeker born every minute."—Firesign Theatre

Serial Killers

A strange phenomenon seems to have been emerging through the 1990s. Since the trials of Richard Ramirez and **Henry Lee Lucas** and the executions of **John Wayne** Gacey and Ted Bundy, the incidence of serial murder has progressively dropped, particularly the spectacular and highly publicized kind that has previously never failed to generate books, films, and even trading cards. At the same time, the public fascination seems to have dwindled, and the sale of paperback serial killer books and other related merchandise has declined. No solid evidence can be clearly produced to demonstrate a correlation between the impulse to commit this kind of crime and the expectation of public, mass-media notoriety. But it does bear considering that life and art—or at least life and tabloid exploitation—are more intertwined than we care to suspect.

Although the serial killers may no longer be the toast of the tabloids, they do still enjoy the admiration of one disturbed section of the community. The death row groupies still compete for the attention of convicted serial killers. At last count, no fewer than six women were claiming to be Richard Ramirez's jailhouse love.

Shaheed

In what amounts to a rerun of Hassan-i-Sabbah and his twelveth-century hashasheens (assassins), young Muslim men, known in Arabic as the Shaheed, are prepared to die for Allah and the political objectives of the fundamentalist Hamas terror group. Strapping explosives to their bodies, they commit suicide by blowing themselves up on crowded streets or in public buildings with the intention of taking as many of the infidels with them as possible. They are likely to become the spearhead of any future campaign of psychological warfare against Israel and the U.S. To become Shaheed requires a lengthy preparation process, the culmination of which is a ceremony to overcome the fear of death. The Shaheed recruit is taken to a cemetery where he lies alone between gravesites for long hours. The recruits—mainly nondescript young men who are devout Muslims with no distinguishing features and no criminal records—are also told that they will be honored in heaven with all that they desire, including seventy-two beautiful virgins. In addition, by his death, the assassin-to-be will pave the way to heaven for members of his family who come after him.

Shark Attack

In what appears to be yet another symptom of the reality of global warming, large and potentially man-eating sharks have started to boldly go where no shark has gone before. In September of 1998, a great white attacked a surfer off the coast of Southern California, while earlier in the same year another great white went after a cabin cruiser in the Adriatic near Ancona, Italy. Naturalists claim that changes in water temperature have radically altered shark migration and feeding patterns, and large sharks are now liable to appear where never previously seen.

Sirhan Sirhan

Ever in the shadow of JFK, Robert Kennedy has remained the little brother. Even his assassination, although hardly unnoticed, has never amassed quite the wealth of speculation, theory, and detailed examination that surrounds the murder of his elder brother. In the same way, Sirhan Sirhan—the supposed lone nut who gunned down Bobby on June 5, 1968, in the kitchen of the Ambassador Hotel in Los Angeles after the Senator and presidential candidate delivered his victory speech in the California Democratic Primary—has never been as seriously scrutinized as Lee Harvey Oswald. On the surface, it would seem that Sirhan—a Palestinian refugee who claimed to have shot Bobby because he was "furious over the plight of Palestinian Arabs"—was perfect lone nut material. As with the **JFK assassination**, a number of anomalies in the LAPD handling of the situation and an immediate **CIA** presence on the scene very quickly created doubts in a public mind already traumatized by the previous killing in Dallas. Stories circulated that the number of bullets recovered from the scene exceeded the maximum eight rounds in Sirhan's revolver, and that the reported rate of fire was higher than would have been possible with just one shooter. Again, as in the case of JFK, a large amount of crucial evidence and eyewitness testimony seems to have mysteriously disappeared, including a sequence of pictures taken of Bobby as he was actually being shot.

One piece of the story that seems to have been deliberately suppressed—both by the LAPD and the CIA agents who were quickly on the scene—is the presence of "the polka-dot woman." A number of witnesses insist that they saw Sirhan in the company of a young woman in a polka-dot dress during the time right before the shooting. LAPD Sergeant Paul Scharaga, the first supervising officer to arrive at the Ambassador, was sufficiently convinced by these stories and issued an all-points-bulletin for her, only to find himself confronted by an unexplained, twenty-minute police radio blackout. When communications were restored, Detective Inspector John Powers showed up and ordered Scharaga to cancel the APB. The sergeant refused, but Powers went over his head and the APB was cancelled anyway.

Later, Lieutenant Manuel Pena, the officer in charge of preparing the Sirhan case for trial—an officer with alleged CIA connections—was accused by conspiracy researchers of deliberately directing the attention of investigators away from the question of the woman in the polka-dot dress. This perceived cover-up, and the fact that Sirhan has always claimed to have no memory of the actual shooting, has given rise to the repeated suspicion that far from being a lone nut, Sirhan Sirhan was a brainwashed, robot killer of the kind that the CIA's **MKULTRA** group was attempting to create. The theory was, then, that the "polka-dot woman" was his agency handler.

Snuff Movies

The legend of the snuff movie describes the genre as amateur or quasi-professional film or videotape in which a victim—usually an attractive young man or woman—is killed oncamera for no other reason than the vicarious and terminally perverse pleasure of the audience. These films have been around since the late 1960s, yet despite lengthy searches, one could not be located. The first snuff movie tales told how short films, supposedly made in Mexico or Honduras and showing unsuspecting prostitutes or rent boys being gratuitously murdered, were shipped north to Los Angeles, at great expense, to be shown at private parties for decadent movie stars and Hollywood moguls. Roman Polanski was reputed to have a collection, as was Mama Cass Elliot, but she burned hers in the aftermath of the Sharon Tate murders.

The second phase came in the form of accusations that various Satanic cults made videos of ritual human sacrifices and then circulated them on the deepest blackmarket. In 1976, *Snuff*, an Anglo/Argentinean production directed by Allan Shackerton, included footage purported to come from an Argentinean snuff movie called *Slaughter*. The promo slogan screamed "filmed in South America where life is cheap," but the included footage was so singularly unconvincing and plainly phoney that patrons actually asked for their money back because they hadn't witnessed a genuine murder. *Snuff* finished up doing the rounds of fleapits and drive-ins, double billed with a Farley Granger movie titled *The Slasher*.

The concept of snuff movies again reared its ugly head in the 1980s, when the religious right, Andre Dworkin, members of Women Against Pornography, and **Reagan** Attorney General Ed Meece all treated snuff movies as absolute fact. They cited them as evidence of the ultimate evil created by a sexually permissive and uncensored society.

Even in the 1990s, where almost everything can be obtained with minimal difficulty, where Web sites show images of dead bodies, where the 8mm home movies of the SS circulate by neo-Nazi mail-order, and the video series *Faces of Death*—collections of various kinds of death on camera—can be rented in most video stores, still no snuff movies appeared. Although people continue to insist that they really exist, that "a friend of a friend…etc., etc.," real proof remains elusive. Hopefully, the snuff movie is a terminal fantasy rather than a damning reality, and maybe we're not quite as bad as we think we are.

Soviet Nukes

When the Soviet Union collapsed and the Berlin Wall came down, the world breathed a sigh of relief that the specter of nuclear war had retreated by a couple of paces. News currently leaking out of Russia, however, seems to indicate that perhaps relief was a little premature. According to the *Washington Post* and other sources, Russia possesses 7,000 nuclear warheads mounted on missiles in permanent readiness for launching at the U.S. and Western Europe. It also has 5,000 fully deployed tactical nukes without locking devices to prevent their use. An additional 12,000 weapons are in storage, protected by an Army that is frequently as much as six months behind on paying its troops. As Russia's economic and political meltdown worsens, the threat of one or more Russian nukes—or even raw, weapon-grade **plutonium**—falling into the hands of either terrorists or some extremist faction grows more acute.

A worse danger, though, may lurk in the possibility of an accidental nuclear detonation. In the **nuclear near miss** of 1995, an all-out nuclear strike was only averted by a Moscow minute. Since that crisis, other "prepare to launch" orders have mysteriously been issued for no apparent reason and then countermanded before they could be acted upon. In February 1997, scientists at the Impulse State Scientific Production Association—the body responsible for command and control of the huge Russian nuclear arsenal—went on strike because their salaries hadn't been paid for eight months. Russian Defense Minister Igor Rodionov was forced to admit he couldn't guarantee security of the country's weapons. Even the control systems on the Russian missiles may be seriously deteriorated to the point of not functioning properly, as funds are not available for their maintenance and overhaul. If one of them should be launched, where it lands could be anyone's guess.

Specter, Arlen

Senator Arlen Specter may have enjoyed one of the stranger rises to power in the annals of U.S. politics. He first came to major public attention when, as a thirty-three-year-old Philadelphia lawyer, he was invited to serve as counsel for the Warren Commission probing the **assassination of President John F. Kennedy**. It was Specter who devised the "magic bullet theory," the idea much derided by New Orleans DA Jim Garrison both in real life and as played by Kevin Costner in the Oliver Stone movie *JFK*. The theory was that a single bullet, supposedly fired by Lee Harvey Oswald, managed to zigzag through the president's body and then exit to strike Texas Governor **John Connally** in the wrist.

As with so many others who worked for the Warren Commission (including Gerald Ford, who got to be president for a couple of years and pardon Richard Nixon), Arlen Specter used the contacts he made through the Warren Commission as a springboard to public office. He started as Philadelphia District Attorney and eventually made it to the Senate. In 1991, he again came to the public's notice for his near abusive questioning of Anita Hill during the Senate Confirmation Hearings that gave Clarence Thomas a seat on the U.S. Supreme Court. In 1996, Specter considered a run for the presidency but dropped out after the first Republican primaries.

One of Specter's more bizarre escapades, however, is only known to collectors of **Elvis Presley** trivia. It took place in 1977. Specter was fresh out of office after serving as Philadelphia District Attorney. He may have needed a boost of publicity. Four days before Elvis died, a psychic named Marc Salem wrote a prediction of Presley's death, including the headlines from both the *Philadelphia Daily News*, "The King Is Dead" and the *Philadelphia Inquirer*, "The King Dies At 42." Salem placed the written predictions in an aspirin bottle that was then baked into a pretzel. The entire weird event was supervised by no less than Arlen Specter. It's to such men that we give power in this democracy.

Spielberg, Steven

One of the stranger rumors out on the edge of the secret government/alien control mindset is that movie director and Hollywood mogul Steven Speilberg is, in fact, collaborating with extraterrestrial beings and working for an alien takeover as an associate of the ultra-secret human/alien liaison group **MJ12**. Extreme UFO buffs claim his film *Close Encounters of the Third Kind* is, in fact, a fictionalized but highly accurate account of the 1954 alien landing in the California desert near Muroc Air Base where the aliens first revealed themselves to representatives of the U.S. and other governments. The argument continues that movies like *Close Encounters* and *ET* are really part of a psychological mass softening up program, preparing the people of Earth for the day when the aliens will finally go public and show us who's really running things.

Stalin's Bedroom

Although it is impossible to verify, this story has been circulating in Russia since the de-Stalinization of the Soviet Union in the late 1950s. Seemingly, the notorious dictator, a man who was directly responsible for the deaths of millions of people, felt highly insecure if he couldn't sleep in his own familiar bedroom. Obviously, this was very difficult for the head of a superpower whose official duties involved a great deal of traveling. To solve what might seem to be this obsessive-compulsive problem, Stalin ordered that hundreds of exact replicas of his bedroom be constructed all over the Soviet Union, so he was able to maintain the illusion that he was home at bedtime.

Stealth

Although the United States Air Force is unwilling to give either a confirmation or a categorical denial, rumors are gaining momentum that the radar-confusing stealth systems used in the ultra-secret Stealth Fighter and Stealth Bomber do not work when the outside of the aircraft is wet. Flying through clouds or rain, the revolutionary black airplanes are easily detectable on radar. The radar simply sees the configuration of water droplets on the outer surface of the plane. If this is true, it means that the U.S. taxpayer has dug deep to the tune of many billions of dollars for yet another massively costly weapons system that, while looking sexy, is totally useless. It also tends to negate the stories that stealth is an alien technology given to us ignorant earthlings by ETs in return for the government allowing them to abduct and conduct medical experiments on the unsuspecting public. Unless, of course, the little grey suckers were pulling a con on the gullible Pentagon.

Sverdlovsk Midget

Among the alleged KGB secret files that have been sold on the Russian **UFO black market** since the break up of the Soviet Union are both film and documents relating to an incident that was seemingly code-named the "Sverdlovsk Midget." It is being heralded as the "Russian **Roswell**." As far as the story can be pieced together, it appears that in November of 1968, a cluster of four bright objects were seen over a remote forest area relatively near the city of Sverdlovsk, east of the Ural Mountains. Observers, who included the police and military, reported that three of the objects maintained a steady flight pattern, but a fourth suddenly lost altitude and dropped out of sight. Some also claimed that after the fourth object fell away, they saw a flash like an explosion near the ground.

In early 1969, after the spring thaw, a crew of loggers working in the forest came across a half-buried disc-shaped object, twenty-five to thirty feet in diameter, just inside the trees by a cleared area. One piece of black market film is color footage of a squad of soldiers guarding the object, which appears to be constructed from a greyish metal and looks a lot like the conventional image of a flying saucer. Meanwhile, it is inspected by military officers and civilians with a distinctly authoritative KGB air about them. The accompanying documentation states that after securing the object, technical and biological material was removed and ultimately sent to Moscow for analysis.

Another filmed sequence, also in color, shows three men and one woman, wearing white lab coats and surgical gloves, in a room that has been positively identified as an operating room in what is now the Moscow Medical Institute. At the time, it was also the much less accesible Scientific Research Institute for Biology. They appear to be dissecting the remains—a single arm and a section of torso—of a humanoid creature with greenish skin, approximately four feet tall. This was presumably the midget referred to in the operation's code name. Experts who have examined the film are satisfied that the instruments and surgical practices shown are consistent with those in use at the time. The film stock and other details conform to products used by military and government filmmakers in the late 1960s. Because a modern forgery can all but be ruled out, the major question that remains is: Are we looking at some bizarre piece of KGB disinformation, or did the Soviet Union actually have in its possession an alien spacecraft and the remains of at least one of its occupants? And if so, where are they now?

Symbionese Liberation Army

Like Jim Jones and **The People's Temple**, the Symbionese Liberation Army's (SLA) kidnapping of heiress Patti Hearst and their demise in a shoot-out with the LAPD would probably have become nothing more than a mere footnote to history, the self-destructive last stand of 1960s radicalism in its desperate death throes. But it continues to crop up as a cross-reference for various conspiracy theories centered around the ongoing possibility of government mind control. The alleged story of SLA leader Donald DeFreeze, also known by his guerrilla code name Cinque, is often cited as a textbook case of the mind-controlled killer zombie let loose to do the bidding of the **CIA** or some more shadowy agency.

In the beginning, De Freeze was nothing more than a snitch, an informant for the LAPD's Criminal Conspiracy Section, giving information on black militant organizations in the late 1960s. In this capacity, he almost certainly had contact with other domestic spy organizations mobilized against the radical left, like Operation Chaos and the FBI's COINTELPRO.

In 1971, DeFreeze was doing time in California's Vacaville Prison when he became an inmate on the notorious "third floor" where CIA drug experiments were alleged to take place. DeFreeze became a test subject and also recruited others under the cover of leading a self-help group called the Black Cultural Association. DeFreeze's own statement is that he was drugged and conditioned by CIA agents and instructed that he would become "the leader of a radical movement and kidnap a wealthy person." After escaping through a conveniently unlocked exit door, DeFreeze did exactly that.

T

Teen Witchcraft

Just as we thought heavy metal rock 'n' roll Satanism was fading away, a new piece of juvenile occultism rears its phantasmagoric head. Perhaps partially inspired by movies like *The Craft*, increasing numbers of teenage girls are apparently embracing the "white magic" of the Wicca religion. Certainly there seem to be enough of them to warrant a lady with the unlikely name of Silver RavenWolf to write a how-to book for teenage witches, *Teen Witch: Wicca for a New Generation*. In the October 1998 issue of the magazine *New Worlds of Mind and Spirit*, Ms. RavenWolf answers readers' questions.

> *Q:* I'm afraid to do ritual because I think that I may conjure something I shouldn't. What should I do?
> *RavenWolf:* You can't conjure things you don't call. No demon will appear looming in the dark...Let's say you find a book that has cool writing, but you can't read the words. Don't use it. Never work with material that you don't comprehend.

On the matter of parental control, RavenWolf is unequivocally firm:

> Your parents, whether you like it or not, do have a say about what adults you associate with or activities in which you chose involvement. Because of the guardianship laws, 95 percent of adult Crafters will not teach witchcraft to minors unless those children live in magickal homes. If your parents don't like or understand the craft and don't like you learning about the craft, they can legally stop you.

It should not be forgotten that teen witches have caused a good deal of trouble down the centuries, the two most obvious examples are the Salem witch trials and the female hippie runaways in the Manson Family.

Telescreens

The idea of telescreens was first presented by George Orwell in his novel *1984*. While viewers watched TV, the TV could also be watching them in the most intrusive, Big Brother surveillance of a civilian population ever conceived. According to writer Alex Constantine, the use of mass spying by telescreens was considered and researched by the U.S. government on at least two occasions. The first was during the Truman administration in 1948. A joint intelligence-community research effort with the code name Operation Octopus (not to be confused with the Octopus Theory) attempted to devise a system that would turn any TV set into a transmitter with a range of twenty-five miles through which agents could pick up audio and video images. The insurmountable glitch in the system was that it had no "wake-up" capability to turn it on when something interesting was happening. Monitoring agents would be forced to watch hours and hours of empty rooms and families idly staring at the TV.

The concept of the telescreen was revived during the Nixon presidency when the Office of Science and Technology (OST) again recommended the use of it for mass surveillance. This time, the right to privacy was saved by

Congressman William Moorhead, who publicly blew the whistle on the plan for the "manufacture and installation of special FM receivers in every home radio and television set, boat and automobile, which could be automatically turned on by the government to contact every citizen whether awake or asleep."

Tesla, Nikola

Croatian-born Nikola Tesla was a genius of the highest order. It is beyond dispute that he was the last of the great Victorian solo inventors who could create radical technological change without the backing of the military or a giant multinational conglomerate. His main claims to fame are that he conceived and made possible alternating current and invented the Tesla coil. But it is also a matter of historical record that he filed literally thousands of patents for revolutionary electrical devices. Few would argue that he was a highly strange individual, with few friends, no known sex life, and an innate ability to visualize everything from lengthy equations to complex pieces of machinery without needing to resort to blackboard or notepad. He also had an almost obsessive affection for New York City pigeons, always carrying breadcrumbs with which to feed them.

When Tesla arrived in New York in 1884 with nothing but a few cents, a letter of introduction to Thomas Edison, and the idea for alternating current, he was welcomed by Edison and given a job. Edison, however, at this point was so wedded to the less practical system of direct current that although he had Tesla design him a number of dynamos, he essentially wasted Tesla's talents. Edison so consistently shortchanged him financially that when offered a joint Nobel Prize for Physics with Edison in 1912, Tesla turned it down, refusing to be associated with his former employer.

Tesla's next patron was George Westinghouse, who made a fortune inventing the railroad airbrake and was moving into the field of electricity. Westinghouse believed implicitly in the AC system and paid Tesla a flat fee of $100,000 for his patents—a deal that would ultimately prove disastrous for Tesla, who seemed to have had little clue about money. Westinghouse put him in complete charge of the ambitious Niagara Falls power station, which proved to be the supreme engineering project of the time.

Where Tesla fact and Tesla mythology begin to separate is at the moment, after the Niagara Falls power house was up and running, that Tesla went to work on what was reputedly the project most close to his heart—the concept of broadcast power. The idea that electrical power could be broadcast through the air like radio waves made absolute sense to a logical mind like Tesla's, but Westinghouse and the other investors he approached were horrified. Why would anyone want to broadcast power? Such a delivery system would, by definition, be without cost to the consumer, and how could that be in a capitalist society? To the money men, the whole project sounded uncomfortably like a form of techno-Bolshevism. It was at this point that the story of Nikola Tesla enters the realm of the everlasting light bulb and the car that ran on tap water, only in his case it goes a quantum leap further.

Tesla did, in fact, get to test his broadcast power system. He found the backing to erect a 200-foot mast atop an 80-foot tower in the Rocky Mountains. The mast was capped by a copper ball, and when the system was powered up, the ball threw off crashing lightning bolts. Specially connected light bulbs, some many miles away, began to glow, but then everything went dark. The Colorado Springs Electric Company had agreed to supply all the power that Tesla needed, but his prototype still managed to burn out the largest generating plant west of the Mississippi.

No doubt exists that Tesla invented a number of functional remote control and robot devices and the carbon button lightbulb that burned with no power input. From there on, the inventions credited to Tesla get much more fanciful. Did Tesla design robot aircraft and submarines prior to World War I only to have them rebuffed by Washington? Did Tesla build a **deathray**, and was the 1908 **Tunguska explosion** a result of a miscalculation on his part? Did Tesla work on anti-gravity devices, and is his work still continuing inside **Area 51**? Did he cooperate with Albert Einstein on the notorious **Philadelphia Experiment**, in which the warship Eldridge was accidentally moved through time? Did he design a non-nuclear doomsday device that would make war impossible?

Much of the speculation over what Nikola Tesla knew and did was fueled by the fact that after he died in poverty on January 7, 1943, in a cheap New York hotel, the FBI showed up in a matter of hours and seized all of his papers, notebooks, and journals in the "interests of national security." They are now classified as "missing" and cannot be obtained through the Freedom of Information Act.

It is ironic that the memory of one of the greatest minds of the twentieth century should become inseparably linked with some of the same century's most outlandish paranoias. The extent of these paranoias can be gauged by "Commander X," an alleged ex-intelligence officer who is anonymously prominent in the field of UFO theory. "X" claims that Tesla was a stranded alien, presumably using the primitive human technology at his disposal, if not to build an escape craft, at least to phone home. Unfortunately, this is a scenario very close to a classic *Star Trek* episode in which Spock is stranded on twentieth-century Earth and creates a time machine out of old radio parts.

Texas Coup, The

In Gore Vidal's autobiography *Palimpsest*, the novelist/screenwriter/actor/wit recounts how John F. Kennedy had a dream-premonition that he would be brought down by a "Texas coup" led by Vice President Lyndon Johnson.

This Gun for Hire

According to the FBI, contract murder has become a growth industry over the last two decades. At least 5,000 professional hits were carried out in the U.S. in 1997 as opposed to a mere 1,000 in 1980. A how-to book titled *The Assassin* has sold over 50,000 copies and become the subject of lawsuits brought by the families of victims. Bureau spokesman Tom Masters explains, "the rise has been caused by tougher divorce laws, which force the guilty party to fork out more money." The current rate for an assassination is between $5,000 and $10,000, and for spouses who might lose millions in a divorce settlement, it has become an attractive option. On the other side of the coin, most middle-class customers don't have a clue about how to deal with a hit man or verify that he can do what he claims. A real professional, the guy the mob might use, gets paid at least $100,000 a job.

Thomas, Chan

Chan Thomas is one of the few End-of-the-World prophets of catastrophe who bases his doomsaying on scientific theory rather than psychic or religious portents. His theories—postulated in his book *The Adam and Eve Story*—are based on the work of Swedish physicist Hannes Alfven. In the mid-1950s, Alfven claimed that semi-liquid bodies act in different ways, depending on the strength of the **magnetic** field in which they find themselves. A container of mercury in a high magnetic field moves with all the properties of a solid block. Reduce the magnetic field and the mercury starts to behave like a less stable liquid. The Earth is a semi-liquid body, and at certain points in space it encounters areas where the magnetic fields are greatly reduced. In one of these magnetic "null zones," the Earth's liquid interior becomes unstable, and the solid outer crust may momentarily torque out and spin in the opposite direction.

According to Thomas, in this context a moment is all it takes. The seas are hurled from their accustomed beds to drown continents with two-hundred-foot tidal waves. Tectonic plates rattle like dice in a crap game, and every volcano in the world blows simultaneously. All but a handful of us are killed instantly, and those who are left have to claw their painful way back to civilization. Thomas sees the biblical Adam and Eve as the survivor memories of a previous disaster of this kind about 12,000 years ago.

Thomas believes that we may be entering one of these magnetic null zones right now. He cites NASA experiments in which lab mice subjected to abnormally low magnetic fields exhibit antisocial behavior, like rape and cannibalism, and then develop massive tumors. Thomas views our current world social upheavals as an indication that we are indeed entering a null gravity zone. Although his vision is depressing, at least he doesn't see an apocalyptic disaster as retribution for bad human behavior; bad human behavior is merely an advance side effect of the apocalypse.

Thule Society

Along with **Ordo Templi Orientis**, the Thule Society was one of the European secret societies to exert a major influence on the embryonic Nazi Party and forge the links between the Nazis and the mystical concepts of racial purity, neo-paganism, and the occult. Many Thulist ideas were incorporated into the quasi-occult structure of the inner core of Himmler's SS, while a leading Thulist, Dr. Frederick Kohn, was responsible for the final design of the Nazi swastika symbol and flag. The ideological difference that eventually split the Thulists from the Nazis and brought about their downfall was their continuing belief in the monarchy, something Hitler would never tolerate, believing as he did that the Hapsburg dynasty betrayed the German people during World War I.

Tinfoil Balls

A frequently repeated rumor during the war in Vietnam was that the Vietcong had perfected a method of confusing the radar of U.S. fighter jets and caused them to crash by firing huge tinfoil balls into the air by means of bungy cords stretched between two trees. When attacking aircraft made low-level strafing runs or dropped napalm from little more than treetop height, the sudden appearance of a metallic object directly in front of them caused the planes' computers to institute immediate evasive action that could flip the aircraft over with disastrous results. It has now become impossible to verify whether the VC weapon, which supposedly cost less than $75, could take out a jet that cost many millions or if the story was a fabricated piece of disinformation disseminated by the anti-war movement of the time.

Topless Donut Diners

In what could only be a philosophical grafting of Homer Simpson and Al Bundy, a number of topless donut diners opened in the early 1990s, primarily along interstate truck routes in the Midwest and the South. The appeal of these joints was that the mainly male customers were served strong, heavily caffeinated coffee and fresh donuts by sub-Hooters girls clad only in short shorts and high heels. In the final year of the Bush administration, churches, the Moral Majority, and local cells of the Christian Coalition moved against this stain on the country's moral escutcheon and attempted to lower the fundamentalist boom on them. The moralists' contention was that such places were a short step from crime and blatant, unregulated prostitution. Many of these dementedly innovative establishments were closed by citizen pressure. Some more tolerant psychologists, though, contended that a downtime interlude of munching chocolate crullers and ogling the breasts of attractive and apparently unbothered young women provided a healthy—if slightly infantile—relief from the prolonged stress of driving a monster twenty-six-wheeler tractor trailer for hours on end.

Tracy, Dick

In its prime, Chester Gould's classic comic strip, *Dick Tracy*, was famous for bizarre and grotesque villains, the two-way wrist radio, and often inexplicable plot lines. Even more inexplicable was the fact that for a number of years, Gould included a small box in the corner of one of the panels of the strip that read, "The nation that controls **magnetism** will rule the universe."

Trenchcoat Mafia, The

Unlike many of the cults and conspiracies examined in this book, the Trenchcoat Mafia, which came to massive media attention after the April

1999 shooting and bombing attack at Columbine High School in Colorado, seems more organic than planned. As far as its origins are concerned, it would seem to be a strange and spontaneous youth cult that grew out of small outsider cliques in mainly suburban high schools who found themselves constantly at war with athletes, fundamentalist Christian kids, and other aggressively straight-arrow elements in the student body. Initially, the Trenchcoat Mafia may have been nothing more than groups of teenagers who embraced the gothic style, with the kind of makeup, ear and nose rings, and tattoo body art that would have created little comment in the larger cities, but in suburbs and small towns could have become the focus of ridicule and harassment.

What would appear to have happened is that when these self-created, stylistic minorities found themselves the butt of continuous verbal and, in some cases, physical abuse, they hardened their attitudes and attempted to present themselves as the ultimate dangerous outsiders. As far as it is possible to trace a phenomenon that occurred in total media isolation, a strange cross-fertilization began to occur, one that might flippantly be described as "Dracula meets *A Clockwork Orange*." The Trenchcoat Mafia started to differ from the average fan of the music and shock-style of **Marilyn Manson** or the vampire novels of Anne Rice by their inclusion of elements drawn from the **Militia Movement** and neo-Nazi skinhead groups. Obsessions with high-tech firearms and Vietcong-style homemade munitions became dangerous elements in the mix. Paint gun war games and World War II battle reenactments started to be part of weekend recreations. Defiant slogans were posted on Trenchcoat Mafia Web pages—"Everything I don't like sucks!" "Stay alive, stay different, stay crazy!" "Don't whimper, it's only a flesh wound!"

The long, black trench or duster coat was not only the garment from which the group derived its name, but also the key to their transformation in attitude. All the way back to the Old West, the long, all-concealing, and sinister duster has been the symbol of the bad guy. It figured prominently and symbolically in spaghetti westerns like Sergio Leone's *Once Upon a Time in the West,* and in the Clint Eastwood canon, especially *High Plains*

Drifter, Pale Rider, and *Unforgiven*. In 1987, it moved into the vampire world in Katherine Bigelow's western-gothic *Near Dark,* and then went on to be almost fetishistically featured in the movies *Highlander, The Crow,* and all their sequels and TV spin-offs. In films like *Last Man Standing,* in Fox TV's **The X-Files** (Agent Mulder's perennial raincoat), and in the 1999 virtual-reality epic *The Matrix,* the long, bat-like, flapping coat seems to have replaced the black leather motorcycle jacket as the standard costume of the dangerous and alienated. Even the venerable Keith Richards adopted one as his own.

As well as a look and a garment, the entertainment industry had already provided more than a few behavioral templates that the Trenchcoat Mafia could put to use. As long ago as 1968, in Lindsay Anderson's classic *If....,* disaffected pupils at a British public school conducted a machine gun massacre of teachers and classmates. In the 1989 dark comedy *Heathers,* the teen rebel character played by Christian Slater (complete with flowing, black raincoat) engaged in high school slaughter, attempting to dynamite his school after murdering a representative selection of cheerleaders and football team heroes. In addition to movies, Japanese *anime* cartoons, comic books like *The Punisher, Spawn,* and *The Preacher,* video games like *Doom,* and the weirdness so readily available at the outer limits of the Internet, all added to the volatile mix, many promoting the impression that death is not only the ultimate sanction, but also something that can be circumvented—and even returned from—by the somber, avenging hero.

It might be possible to dismiss the Trenchcoat Mafia as a localized and short-lived—albeit tragic—aberration, isolated to the Denver area, that will now quickly run its course. This may not, however, be so. According to grapevine reports, on the morning following the Littleton massacre, kids all over the U.S. arrived at school in long, black coats as a defiant act of rebel solidarity, even though many found themselves sent home by authorities or beaten up by their more conservative peers. This must at least prompt the suggestion that a variation of the Trenchcoat Mafia may be the face of youth revolt at the opening of the new millennium.

Tri-lateral Commission

Of the big three international shadow government conspiracy targets—the **Bilderburg Group**, the **Council for Foreign Relations**, and the Tri-lateral Commission, the latter is the newest and most recently formed. Created in the early 1970s with the declared intent of strengthening and defending America's traditional political and economic ties with Europe and Japan, it has been tagged by conspiracists as yet another front for, the **Bavarian Illuminati**, or both. It is regularly accused of being a World Government-in-waiting. More speculation has centered around the fact that many Tri-lateralists are also members of the Council for Foreign Relations. The best known of these are, of course, Jimmy Carter and his security advisor, Zbigniew Brzezinski, whose 1970 statement regarding the future of the world is often quoted as a hidden promotion of the NWO or maybe even a veiled threat: "The world is not likely to unite behind a common ideology or a super-government. The only practical hope is that it will now respond to a common concern for its own survival."

Trinity 3D

Should it bother us that in the privacy of their own homes, an increasing number of people are staring from armchairs and couches through 3D glasses at videocassettes of atomic explosions? Is this a weird twenty-first-century version of gazing into the fire, except that now it is the ultimate planet-consuming fire of nuclear holocaust? This bizarre and scary image is conjured by the commercials that, through 1997–98, have proliferated on late-night cable TV between the tele-psychics and the 900 numbers for phone sex. *Trinity 3D—The Atomic Bomb Movie* is the latest in a series of nuclear explosion videos being sold by mail and TV advertising. They seem to be coming from the same kind of production companies and mail-order operations that also supply videos of crashing planes, Hitler, wild animals eating each other, fatal accidents captured on film, women firing automatic weapons, outtakes from *The Jerry*

Springer Show, and the notorious sequence of a woman being killed by an oncoming train that so delights Howard Stern. These productions are strictly short-attention-span fare, with no plot line or even documentary-style continuity, and their major appeal seems to be the simple prurient shock value of the basic and often repeated images. In this, their nearest kissing cousins would be the ever-popular sexual pornography with perhaps some distant historic roots in the public hangings of the eighteenth and nineteenth century. Could it be that getting off by staring at the gruesome, strange, and unthinkable may well become a new definition of video porno?

Tunguska Explosion, The

Around 7 A.M. on June 30, 1908, passengers on the Trans-Siberian Express were amazed by the spectacle of a vast fireball heading in an easterly direction, leaving a bright tail and moving erratically. Moments later, a huge explosion lit up the sky so brightly that it was visible in London, England. The sky remained bright for the next three or four nights. The explosion took place in an area of Northern Siberia known as Tunguska, a remote wilderness of marshes and swampy forest, and was estimated to be the equivalent of a 40-megaton nuclear device. It was some 200 feet across at ground zero, and trees burned for weeks afterwards, destroying some 400 square miles of forest. Fish died in rivers for a number of the following years. Although many of the characteristics of the explosion seemed similar, in future hindsight, to a nuclear detonation—albeit almost forty years before its time—recent post-Soviet expeditions to the area found no traces of radiation but also no sign of meteor fragments.

The Tunguska explosion is one of the major unnatural phenomena of the twentieth century. Explanations include the crash of a large alien spacecraft, the impact of a 100,000-ton asteroid that was vaporized on impact, and the Earth's collision with a piece of anti-matter that mysteriously entered our universe. Perhaps the strangest explanation, though, is that the Tunguska explosion was the result of **Nikola Tesla** testing his rumored **deathray**. According to this scenario, Tesla, discharging a first long-range test shot from the experimental weapon—which used the earth's **magnetic** field as a source of power—had intended for it to produce a harmless detonation in space over the North Pole. Firing it from his private research center on Long Island, New York, he had not allowed for what Einstein mathematically predicted in 1905, that passage through the gravitational field of the Earth would produce a slight downward curvature of the ray, enough for it to fall short and hit Northern Siberia.

Turner Diaries, The

This novel by Dr. William Pierce, a former assistant professor of physics at Oregon State University and leader of the right-wing National Alliance, is the story of courageous Americans saving their country from the conspiracies of mongrel races. It has been adopted as a blueprint, mindset, and ultimate goal of white supremacist and armed **militia** groups all over the country. With its embrace of the book, the militant right joins the ranks of the **Heaven's Gate** cultists, **Scientologists**, and the Manson Family, who all embody works of science fiction in their philosophy.

TWA-800

Since TWA flight 800 went down over Long Island, New York, on the night of July 17, 1996, killing all 230 passengers and crew, a number of both official and unofficial explanations have been offered for the disaster. One of the most recent official pronouncements, however, seems to have grim ramifications for the traveling public. On the day of the crash, ten U.S. military aircraft were operating in the area, and some crash investigators are convinced that powerful radar or radio pulses from the military jets burned out the 747's electrical circuits, causing the tail to swing violently or perhaps trigger fuel explosions. The U.S. National Transportation Safety Board has yet to make an official ruling, but its chairman, James Hall, admits that the new theory is "feasible," and that would mean all military aircraft would have to be treated as a threat to civilian flights.

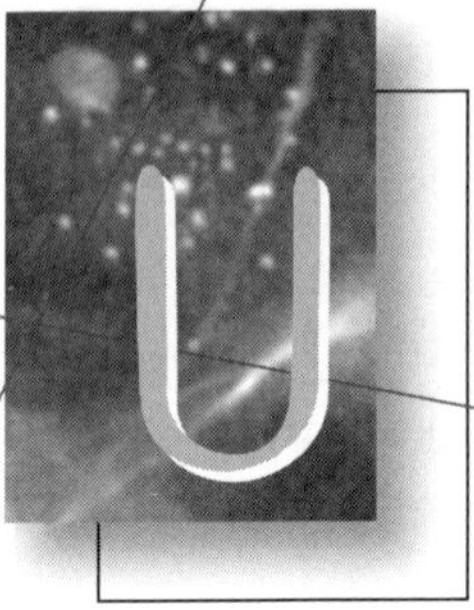

UFO Black Market

The chaos that is the result of the Russian transformation from communism to capitalism has proved a boon for UFO researchers. In an environment where, as one black marketeer was quoted on CNN, "everything is for sale in the new Russia," a trade in "liberated" KGB documents relating to UFOs and similar phenomena has become an underground growth industry. So far, this material has included files, documents, photographs, and even a film quickly purchased and aired by the TNT cable network of a crashed UFO and a Soviet alien autopsy that has been given the code name "The **Sverdlovsk Midget**."

One of the immediately striking aspects of the material that has come out of the Soviet files is that it parallels reports collected over the years by private UFO researchers in the West. Although the stories were never made public in the way that they were on the other side of the Iron Curtain, it would appear that Soviet citizens were also experiencing what they firmly believed were **alien abductions**, virtually identical to the ones described by their counterparts in Europe and America—right down to implanted objects, missing time, memories of strange medical procedures, and (yes) even the celebrated **anal probe**.

Three possible alternatives seem to exist regarding this bonanza for UFOlogists. The first is that the supposed KGB files and films are fabrications that the Russian Mafia is more than happy to sell to crazy Westerners for prices that seem to run in the $10,000 range. The second is that the material truly originates from the KGB, but it is part of some bizarre disinformation operation that was never implemented. The third is that the material is simply genuine. Even before the end of the Cold War, the **CIA** was well aware that the Soviets had a major interest in UFOs, and the authorities would reward informants who came forward with accounts of UFO sightings. A number of reports in the 1940s and early 1950s clearly indicated that Joseph Stalin was fascinated—and decidedly paranoid—at the idea that extraterrestrials might be visiting the Earth. It was also well documented that Russian UFO reports were collated and analyzed by an organization known as the Commission on Anomalous Phenomena, whose work appears to have been discontinued after the fall of communism.

Universal Sign of the Donut

The Universal Sign of the Donut is recommended as an initial greeting to all possible extraterrestrials and other beings of doubtful planetary origin. Extend the right arm so it is straight out in front of the body. The right hand should be slightly below shoulder level with the palm down, the index and second finger extended, the thumb beside the index finger, and the other two fingers folded back (much the same hand configuration as the Pope uses when blessing his followers). Starting upward in a counterclockwise direction, draw an invisible circle about ten inches in diameter in midair. You have made the Universal Sign of the Donut.

UPUAUT 2

In April of 1993, a small robot called UPUAUT 2, scarcely larger than an ultra-high-tech roller skate, opened an entire new can of worms regarding the age, origin, and purpose of the Great Pyramid. The robot accomplished this by simply starting up a narrow shaft deep inside the Great Pyramid at Giza as part of an internal survey project. For the first eighty-four inches, the shaft ran horizontally but then turned up at an angle of almost forty degrees. The team controlling the robot, a research group from the German Archeological Institute in Cairo, led by engineer Rudolf Gantenbrink, watched its forward progress on a TV monitor that fed images down a trailing cable. Great care was taken that UPUAUT 2 did not become wedged, as the passage was no more than eight inches square in cross section. If the robot did become stuck, retrieval was impossible. In ancient Egyptian, "upuaut" means the "opener of the ways," but the machine had no way of breaking itself free.

UPUAUT 2 continued to climb for a further 130 feet. The shaft was straight and regular, the walls and floor precision smooth. Although the Great Pyramid had been subject to both earthquakes and centuries of human vandalism, it was surprisingly uncluttered by debris. As the robot approached the 130-feet mark, an object became visible on the monitor. A metal plate had been set in the floor. Unfortunately, UPUAUT 2 had no equipment to lift the plate or test its composition. The obvious assumption was that it had to be made of copper because that was the only metal widely available in 2550 BC, during the reign of the Pharaoh Khufu, when the Great Pyramid was supposedly built. How the plate was positioned there or what its purpose might have been were two mysteries that hardly fit with the prevailing theory that the passageway up which UPUAUT 2 was moving was nothing more than a simple airshaft.

The robot rolled across the plate and continued for another 210 feet. At this point, it encountered a second, and this time, truly sensational find. UPUAUT 2 could go no further because it had reached a door, a limestone slab with two metal handles fitted in it that seemed to be the remains of a mechanism for opening and closing it. The whole idea that shafts with opening and closing access doors, far too small for a man to crawl through, that must have been built as part of the express design of the pyramid was radical to the point of mind-boggling. They could not have been bored or cut through the layers of stone with any kind of hand-operated device available to the ancient Egyptians. Did it mean that the Great Pyramid, far from being the burial place of a truly megalomaniac king, was something completely different? Something that needed a complex and controllable airflow system? A strange but sophisticated observatory in which the shafts served as some means of alignment? Or was it something previously unimagined by historians and archeologists? UPUAUT 2's final act before backing down the shaft was to direct the beam of a laser at the bottom edge of the door. The door did not fit absolutely flush to the base of the shaft, indicating that it could be—and had been—raised and lowered, and micromovements of air seemed to indicate that a larger, and previously unknown chamber lay beyond.

When Gantenbrink went public with the data and videotapes from UPUAUT 2, he astonishingly ran into another kind of closed door. The Egyptian authorities withdrew all permits allowing him to work inside the Great Pyramid, and the UPUAUT 2 project was brought to a grinding and highly frustrating halt. The reason for this obstruction was that the orthodox archeological establishment, both in Egypt and the rest of the world, wanted no new rash of bizarre theories regarding the Great Pyramid—no more books claiming it was built by aliens or telekinetic shaman, and definitely no more evidence that threw doubt on the idea that it was nothing more than Khufu's simple, enormous tombstone.

U.S. Postal Service

Why have the postal workers of America gained a reputation for being among the most homicidal, disgruntled group of employees in the world? Why has the postal worker shooting up the sorting office become what seems to be such a common occurrence that it has all but become a media cliche? In his book *Virtual Government*, writer Alex Constantine sees it all as the result of yet another government conspiracy. He lays out the frightening scenario that the Postal Service is being used as a test bed for various forms of behavior modification, employing a combination of psychological techniques, post-hypnotic suggestion, and direct electronic brain stimulation. He cites the 1989 "epidemic" of murders and suicides by postal workers in the San Diego area, during which a half dozen employees either murdered colleagues or killed themselves. It is an example of what he concludes (although with very little solid evidence) was a covert mind-control operation that went wrong. A more cynical view of the matter tends to blame such so-called epidemics on the possibility of overzealous, overbearing, or just plain sadistic supervisors. The fact does remain, however, that if the government is really messing with the minds of our postal workers, it may not be the first time U.S. citizens have been used as experimental guinea pigs without their knowledge or consent. Theorists like Constantine always cite examples like the notorious **MKULTRA** experiments in the mid-1950s, in which LSD was administered to unwitting random subjects, as a basis for the idea that "if they did it once, they can do it again."

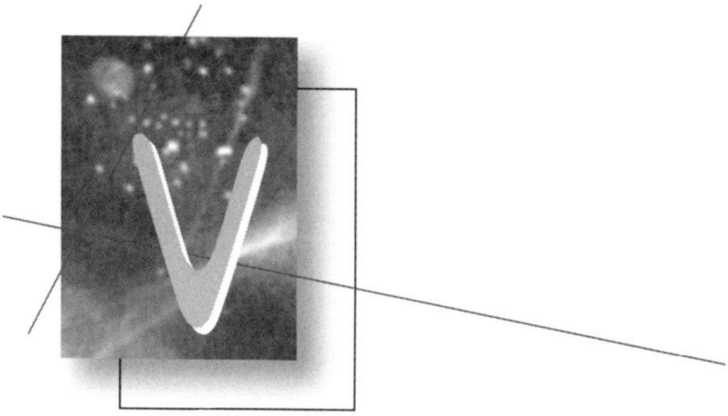

Violent World Syndrome

Professor George Gerbner is one of the very few who have actually studied the long-term effects of TV. For over a quarter of a century, his students at the Annenberg School for Communications at the University of Pennsylvania have monitored shows and logged statistics. Although still largely locked into the specifics of violence, Gerbner does recognize that the perception-warping potential of TV is as important as mere copycat behavior in explaining violence. He has coined the phrase "violent world syndrome." The most obvious example is that while crime figures are actually on a steady if gradual decline, the general perception is that they are rising by quantum bounds. "If you're growing up in a heavy-viewing home, you live in a meaner world—and you act like it—than if you're a neighbor who lives in the same world and watches less television."

Barry Sanders, who teaches a course called "The History of Ideas" at Claremont College, takes the violent world theory a stage further. "We may be inadvertently creating a new kind of human being, generations of kids without imaginations, with the inability to conjure their images because television does it for them. And if that's real, that's amazingly important if we care about anything like hope."

Vultures

Remember the old joke that used to be printed on posters and T-shirts? One vulture looks at another and says "Screw this waiting, I'm going to kill something." It seems the Griffon vulture of Northern Spain has finally made exactly that evolutionary leap and developed the technique of hunting in packs. The first prey of these killer vultures has been young domestic animals such as lambs, calves, and foals. Government officials at first refused to believe stories of the hunting vultures, until photographs were produced showing a group of Griffons surrounding a sheep and using their sharp beaks and powerful necks to peck it to death.

W

Wackenhut, George

George Wackenhut was a former FBI agent who became convinced that his future lay in Bureau techniques for collection and storage of information on as many individuals and organizations as possible. Such materials provided the power base for his hero and mentor, **J. Edgar Hoover**. After leaving the FBI, Wackenhut formed the private security organization that bears his name. Normally, such organizations are prohibited by law from doing contract work for any branch of the federal government. By using his Bureau ties and a previously unnoticed loophole in the law, Wackenhut garnered a number of lucrative contracts providing surveillance, **phone taps**, guard services, and even private jails for various branches of government, including the armed forces. As such, the Wackenhuts constitute what amounts to an independent national police force, free of even the slim restraints that are supposed to limit and control the behavior of the **CIA**, FBI, **DEA**, **NSA**, et al.

One of the major Wackenhut contracts is to provide perimeter security for the notorious **Area 51**, the site outside Nellis Air Force base in

Nevada where ultra-secret and, according to some, alien experimental aircraft are tested. Because Area 51 has become a tourist spot for the **X-Files** mindset, uniformed Wackenhuts have repeatedly come into conflict with the saucer watchers and UFO spotters who try to get as close to Area 51 as possible. Reports from members of the public claim that Wackenhuts have threatened them at gunpoint, confiscated video and camera equipment, and attempted to run vehicles off the road. Seemingly a major concern among those who have experienced these confrontations at Area 51 is the youth of the some of the Wackenhut guards, some being scarcely more than teenagers, who are heavily armed and apparently convinced they are some kind of elite force.

War of the Worlds

If any proof was needed for the extremes to which human beings can go in their imaginations when pushed by unfocused stress and anxiety, we need look no further than Halloween 1938. That was when Orson Welles and the Mercury Theater made their historic, live **CBS** radio broadcast of their dramatic adaptation of H. G. Wells's novel *The War of the Worlds*. In the fall of 1938, the world was an uneasy place. In Europe, the war clouds were gathering, and the Nazis were making their moves on Czechoslovakia and Austria. In the Far East, the armies of Imperial Japan were storming across China. The Spanish Civil War had provided a trailer of horrors to come, and back in the U.S., the Roosevelt New Deal scarcely made a visible dent in the Great Depression. The story of hostile invaders from the planet Mars attacking the Earth and destroying human civilization struck a bizarre chord in the psyches of its listeners on that night of October 31.

The Mercury Theater show was staged as a live news interruption of a scheduled program of dance music, and something in the stressed-out American psyche of the time decided to take it on absolute face value. Long before the one-hour drama ran its course, terrified citizens had grabbed rifles and shotguns and raced out of their houses to confront the invincible Martians, ready to beat them back to their spacecraft or die trying. A number of individuals attempted suicide, and one actually succeeded. The following Monday morning brought recriminations and shamed faces. Consumer labeling of fantasy and science fiction on radio and TV was eventually introduced, and after a major media flurry, life went back to what passed for normal.

Water

Forget food, oil, or living space. Water is so fundamental that it can provide the perfect sneak preview of the horrors just around the corner. In some parts of the world, the tension over water is close to the conflict point. Ignore for a moment how the water tables under the grainfields of the Midwest are being dangerously depleted. Let's just take a look at one of the most significant rivers in history. The Nile was one of the great cradles of human civilization. Right now, Ethiopia is making studies of how it might harness the headwaters of the Blue Nile, and these studies are making the Mubarek government sick to its collective stomach. Already, Ethiopia and the Sudan are demanding a greater share of the Nile waters on which sixty million Egyptians are totally dependent. Egypt almost shut down the Aswan High Dam in 1988 because of low water levels, and the current Ethiopian scheme could reduce Egypt's water supply by 20 percent. Western diplomats are quite certain Egypt will go to war over the Nile water if push comes to shove.

Similar scenarios of those upriver contemplating conflict with those downriver, or neighboring countries who are tapping into the same water table eyeing each other with increasing hostility, are coming to a boil all along the eastern Mediterranean. Libya's Muammar Qaddafi has begun a project of man-made rivers, at a cost of $24 billion, to exploit the deep groundwater under the Sahara. This water resource is unreplenishable and will almost certainly run out around 2020. The wells will not only go dry in Libya but also in Algeria and Morocco. The same applies to the Jordan. Israel and Jordan are each using 15 percent more water every year, and the common belief is that water is like a loaded gun held to Israel's head, and the problem may be insoluble. Turkey's Ataturk Dam on the

Euphrates is threatening to cause water shortages in Iraq and Syria. Couple this with the level of weaponry in any of these countries, and now we're talking apocalypse for real.

Closer to home, if the Hoover Dam on the Colorado River just outside Las Vegas ever collapsed, it would wipe out civilization as we now know it in the desert Southwest. Even without a mishap, continued population expansion in Los Angeles and Las Vegas could cause serious competition for the same water, and the middle of the twenty-first century could see California and Nevada eyeballing each other and perhaps contemplating civil war over water.

Watt, James

While speaking out against environmental controls on the timber industry, specifically the highly destructive clear-cutting of stands of trees in Northern California, James Watt, Secretary of the Interior during **Ronald Reagan**'s first term, made the most amazing statement. There was really no need to worry about the environment because "the second coming of Jesus Christ was close at hand," and presumably after that, it would hardly matter anymore.

Wheaton, Illinois

The town of Wheaton, Illinois, is not only the home of Billy Graham but also boasts the headquarters of Young Americans for Freedom and The Christian Crusade Against Communism.

Wheel of the Dharma

According to millenniumist John Hogue, the Wheel of the Dharma, the Buddhist measure of time, truth, and enlightenment, will grind to a halt sometime around the year 2000. A new Buddha is required to give it a fresh spin every 2,500 years, and the last incarnation of the Awakened One occurred in 500 B.C. Because no new Buddha has appeared to spin the cosmic wheel of fortune, the arithmetic is simple. Another reason not to make too many plans for the year 2001. Open the pod bay door please, HAL.

Women Smoking

As the pressure against cigarette smoking mounts—at least in a majority of Western nations—a bizarre side effect is starting to reveal itself, primarily on the Internet. Since 1997, a number of Web sites have sprung up that feature pictures of women smoking cigarettes. Some of the graphics show models revealingly nude or dressed in lingerie, but others are simply recycled shots of Marlene Dietrich, Lauren Bacall, or Joanna Lumley from the British TV series *Absolutely Fabulous*. In a strange reversal of the contemporary trend for one-time fetish items like leather and rubber clothing, exotic footwear, chains, and handcuffs to become incorporated as part of mainstream fashion, the more the cigarette is legislated against, the more it seems to become an object of inverted desire. Almost as though confirming the pornographic content of the "women smoking" Web pages, some of the large family-oriented Web servers like America Online have blocked easy access. Could it be that we have a new natural law for sociologists, that prohibition will inevitably beget perversion?

Workplace Surveillance

As increasing numbers of corporations make use of advanced electronics to keep watch on their workers, the question has to be asked—when we go to work for an individual or corporation, do we give up all rights to privacy? "Eye in the sky" surveillance cameras over employees handling cash, and the routine logging, timing, and recording of phone calls in telemarketing has been around for some time. Newer wrinkles include devices that centrally monitor e-mail and log the duration of active use of employees' computer terminals and the documents they may be working on. Smart cards—presented as systems for workers' protection—allow access to various areas of the workplace. They also maintain a record of employee movements, including how long they stay in the bathroom. In most high-tech corporations, employees are usually able to outwit at least the in-house checks on their computers by creating ad hoc screening systems that make it appear they're working when they're not. Perhaps this is why rumors still circulate of the nameless Hollywood studio mogul with an income in excess of a hundred million a year who, immediately upon arriving at work each morning, wanders the parking lot, checking the hoods of the cars belonging to his underlings, feeling how warm they are as an indication of how long the help has been at work.

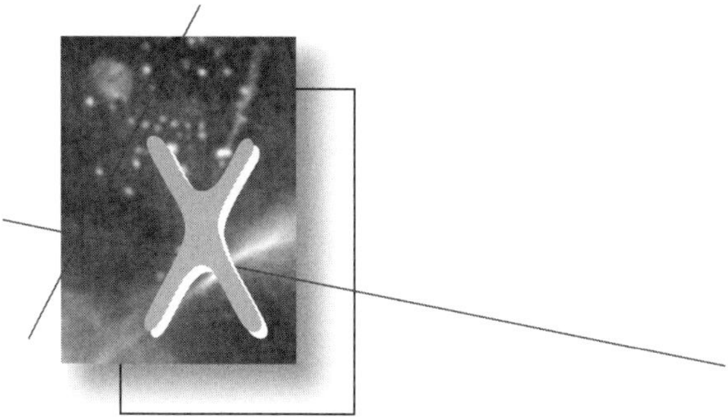

X-Files, The

The long-running TV series and its attendant big-screen movie have been repeatedly hailed by conspiracy buffs as showing, if not the substance of shadowy government dirty tricks (conspiracy buffs can almost never agree on substance), at least the structure of the conspiracy. Indeed, doesn't the backstory of Cancer Man, the long-running archvillain, include being a shooter in the Kennedy assassination? It was probably inevitable that *The X-Files* should attract its own conspiracy theory. Certain archconservatives claim the show is a plot by the Fox network and its owner, Australian press baron Rupert Murdoch, to undermine public trust in the institutions of government.

X-Ray Spex

From the package booklet included with each pair of novelty store X-Ray Spex: "HOW TO BE THE LIFE OF THE PARTY—You can now be able to seemingly see through clothing with X-Ray Spex. This is just one of the thousands of sensational x-ray illusions now made possible for the first time. For laughs, try this howling funny 'stunt' at your very next party or club meeting: Hang up a bedsheet (as illustrated) on a line and put some strong lights behind it. As each victim walks in front of the illuminated sheet, you will get a perfect effect of seeing their bodies through their clothes. Try standing away at different distances such as three feet, five feet, etc. for different illusions. At a closer range, their clothing seems to vanish so you can see the form beneath. At greater distances, the flesh appears to become transparent so you think you are seeing a living skeleton. Everyone will BEG to take turns peeking. Livens up any get together."

Y

Yeti

Even though more and more people are going into the Himalayas these days, there have been no sightings of the Yeti—the large, shaggy, man-like creature that was, until the 1960s, seen with some regularity in mountainous regions of Nepal, India, and Tibet—for almost ten years. One suggested explanation is that the influx of humanity has destroyed the Yeti's already delicately poised habitat, and instead of being rare, it is now totally extinct.

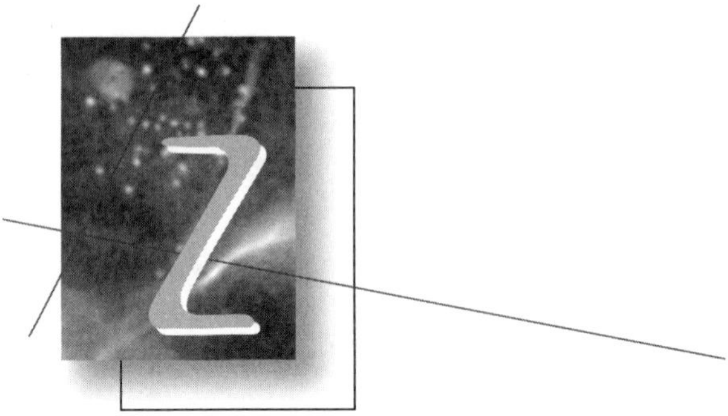

Zapruder Film, The

For years, the 26-second, amateur 8mm home movie shot by Dallas dress manufacturer Abraham Zapruder of the **assassination of President John Kennedy** has been used as documentary support both by advocates of the lone gunman theory and supporters of the various conspiracy concepts. In his 1998 book *Assassination Science*, James Fetzer, a professor of cognitive sciences at the University of Minnesota, makes a persuasive case. He thinks that although the "continuity of the film is preserved well enough to elude all but the most probing eye," the film—maybe the most significant piece of forensic film footage of the twentieth century—was deliberately edited, either by the **CIA**, the FBI, or investigators working for the Warren Commission to conform as much as possible to the Warren Commission's finding that Lee Harvey Oswald acted alone.

Using the relative positions of background spectators and their shadows, position comparisons to the images in various still photographs taken at the time, and most significantly, the seemingly interrupted "blink rate" of a police emergency light reflected in the front grills of both the lead car and the presidential limousine, Fetzer convincingly demonstrates that certain frames have been removed and that the sequence of others has been deliberately changed. Also, retouching has taken place to remove evidence such as the bullet hole in the limousine windshield that could never have happened within the Warren Commission's lone gunman theory of time and number of shots fired.

Certainly, Fetzer's conclusions are enough to swell the numbers of the 70 percent of Americans who already do not accept the findings of the Warren Report, but it also undermines some conspiracy theories whose details are firmly based on a copy of the Zapruder film that was already doctored. One unfortunate side effect of Fetzer's work is that—although he gives the idea no credence—it has resurrected the somewhat dubious idea that the limo driver, Secret Service Agent William Greer, who turned around for an inordinate length of time after the first bullet hit the president, was either the assassin or at least administered the coup de grace with a concealed pistol.

Although Abraham Zapruder died in 1970, his heirs are currently in a major legal dispute with the U.S. government. The heirs have received substantial royalties on usage of the film since it was first shown publicly in the late 1960s. But in 1997, the Assassination Records Review Board declared the film government property and ordered that the ownership be legally transferred. The problem lies in that the feds are refusing to offer more than $3 million for the film and copyright, while the Zapruder estate won't settle for less than $18.5 million. Perhaps the government feels that it put in so much editing work on the film that it deserves some kind of co-credit.

Zeta Reticuli

One of the star systems identified as the home world of the aliens who are causing all the trouble with **abductions**, genetic experiments, and the legendary **anal probe**. Some indications are that the idea might have first been generated in the 1979 movie *Alien*. If you listen carefully to the soundtrack tech babble at the start of the movie, after the crew are awakened prematurely from cryogenic sleep and are trying to find out where they are, a voice mentions that they are in the system Zeta Reticuli.

Zirbel, Craig I.

A latecomer to the ranks of **JFK assassination** theorists, attorney Craig Zirbel points the finger directly at Lyndon Johnson in his 1991 book *The Texas Connection: The Assassination of John F. Kennedy*. It was published in the same year Oliver Stone cryptically suggested the same thing in his movie *JFK* with the question "who benefits?" Zirbel is far from cryptic. He attempts to implicate LBJ with four basic points.

1. Before the shooting, Johnson confided to his longtime mistress, Madeleine Brown, that Kennedy would die during the November visit to Dallas.
2. Johnson headed the team that arranged the route of the JFK motorcade, including the detour through Dealey Plaza.
3. Johnson tried to talk his good buddy Texas governor **John Connally** out of riding in the president's car.
4. After killing Lee Harvey Oswald, Jack Ruby smuggled a letter out of prison that named Johnson as the chief architect of the assassination.

ZOG

The Zionist Occupation Army was the preferred secret government fear fantasy, the assumed source of all ills for neo-Nazis, white supremacists, and the general morass of anti-Semitic, middle-America psychotics during the 1970s and 1980s. In recent years it has largely been displaced by the more all-encompassing sweep of **The New World Order** and a more equal-opportunity hatred.

Bibliography

Books

Adamski, George, with Desmond Leslie, *Inside the Space Ships*, New York, Abelard-Schulman, 1955

Alford, Alan F., *Gods of the New Millennium*, London, Hodder & Stoughton, 1998

Benson, Michael, *Who's Who in the JFK Assassination,* New York, Citadel Press, 1993

Berlitz, Charles, with William Moore, *The Roswell Incident*, New York, Berkley, 1988

Blum, Howard, *Out There*, New York, Pocket Books, 1990

Bly, Nellie, *The Kennedy Men*, New York, Kensington Books, 1996

Brook, Tim, with Earl Marsh, *The Complete Directory of Prime Time Network TV Shows*, New York, Ballantine Books, 1988

Bryan, C. B. D., *Close Encounters of the Fourth Kind*, New York, Knopf, 1995

Constantine, Alex, *Virtual Government*, Venice, CA, Feral House, 1997

Cooper, William, *Behold a Pale Horse*, Sedona, AZ, Light Technology Publishing, 1991

Day, Marcus, *Aliens, Encounters with the Unexpected*, London, CLB International, 1997

Good, Timothy, *Alien Contact*, New York, William Morrow, 1993

Farren, Mick, *The Hitchhiker's Guide to Elvis*, Ontario, Collectors Guide Publishing, 1994

Fetzer, James, *Assassination Science*, Chicago, Catfeet Press, 1998

Keel, John A., *Disneyland of the Gods*, New York, Amok Press, 1988

King, Brian, *Lustmord*, Burbank, Bloat, 1996

Herer, Jack, *The Emperor Wears No Clothes*, Venice, CA, H.E.M.P. Publishing, 1990

Hogue, John, *The Millennium Book of Prophecy*, New York, Harper Collins, 1994

Hopkins, Bud, *Missing Time*, New York, Richard Marek Publishers, 1981

Howard, Michael, *The Occult Conspiracy*, New York, MJF Books, 1989

Lyons, Arthur, *Satan Wants You*, New York, Mysterious Press, 1988

Mack, John E., *Abduction*, New York, Scribners, 1994

Mackay, Charles, *Extraordinary Delusions and the Madness of Crowds*, (first published in 1841) New York, Gordon Press, 1991

Marks, John, *The Search for the Manchurian Candidate*, New York, Norton, 1991

National Insecurity Council, The, *It's a Conspiracy!*, Berkeley, Earthworks Press, 1992

Pozos, Randolfo Rafael, *The Face on Mars*, Chicago, Chicago Review Press, 1986

Randle, Kevin, with Donald R. Schmitt, *UFO Crash at Roswell*, New York, Avon Books, 1991

Reeves, Thomas C., *A Question of Character*, New York, The Free Press, 1991

Sagan, Carl, *The Demon Haunted World*, New York, Random House, 1996

Summers, Montague, *The History of Witchcraft*, New York, Citadel, 1956

Thomas, Chan, *The Adam and Eve Story,* South Chatham, MA, Bengal Tiger Press, 1993

Thomas, Kenn, *Popular Alienation*, Lilburn, GA, Illuminet Press, 1995

Vidal, Gore, *Palimpsest*, New York, Random House, 1995

X, Commander, *Free Energy and the White Dove*, New Brunswick, Abelard Productions, 1992

X, Commander, *Cosmic Patriot Files*, New Brunswick, Abelard Productions, undated

Web Sites

ABC News Web Site
Black Ops Web Site
Black Vault Web Site
Central Intelligence Agency Web Site
Louie Report Web Site
National Security Agency Home Page
Parascope Web Site
Process Web Site
Sightings on the Radio Web Site
The William S. Burroughs Home Page
US Navy Project HAARP Home Page

Periodicals

Alternative Press—February 1997
Covert Action Quarterly—various issues
Delphi Associates Newsletter—various issues
Drug Policy News—various issues
Fortean Times—various issues
International Herald Tribune—various issues
LA Reader—various issues
LA Weekly—various issues
Mondo 2000—various issues
New World of Mind and Spirit—October 1998
Omni—various issues
Science—June 1993
Science Digest—various issues
The Week—various issues
Village Voice—various issues
Wired—various issues

Index

About the Author

Mick Farren is the author of fifteen novels including *The Time of Feasting*, *Necrom*, *Their Master's War*, *The Long Orbit*, and the soon to be published *Jim Morrison's Adventures in the Afterlife*. Among his non-fiction books are *The Black Leather Jacket* and the best-selling *Elvis and the Colonel*. He lives in Los Angeles where he writes for film and TV and teaches a course in science fiction, fantasy, and horror at UCLA. In his spare time, he performs and records rock 'n' roll with his band the Deviants. His studies in the field of the paranormal and alternative history go back to the late 1960s. Since that time, working as a writer and journalist often specializing in the weirder outer limits of popular culture, he has written extensively for magazines like *The Village Voice*, *The Soho Weekly News*, *The LA Reader*, *High Times* and *Rolling Stone*.